Turn Within

Reconnect With Your Inner Peace And Well-Being

The beginning, the quest, the journey, the unveiling, the transformation under progress

Vibha Sharma

*"Man is this wonderful temple in which all the work takes place and the outer world is only a projection of the work done within himself." - **Neville***

Dedication

To my loving and supportive parents...

To

Dear Naurata,

with best o love,

Vish sham

9/7/20

About the Author

My name is Vibha Sharma. I am the Founder and Holistic
Spiritual and Metaphysical Life Coach, Conscious Business
and Mindful Leadership Coach at Cosmicways Holistic Life
Coaching, Global Goodwill Ambassador at Global Goodwill
Ambassadors (GGA), Global Peace Ambassador,
President of India-USA Business Council/Spirituality
Council, WICCI (Women's Indian Chamber of Commerce
and Industry) and San Francisco Chapter Chairperson for
Mindfulness, ALL (All Ladies League) USA, the world's
largest all-inclusive international women's chamber and a
universal movement for the welfare, wealth, and well-being
of all by empowering women leadership.

I believe that every problem has a spiritual solution, and a sense of separation from the Creator/Spirit Self is the cause and root of all human suffering. The most important purpose in this rare, sacred life is your Spiritual Evolution, and this is what Holistic Spiritual and metaphysical Life Coaching is all about. It's a collaborative and empowering process that helps clients identify and articulate their goals and desires. Moreover, it takes into account their physical, spiritual, mental, and emotional needs and helps them achieve those goals by making a viable action plan.

I guide my clients into their holistic journey of self-discovery and conscious living. I help them rise above the mental chaos and noise to a natural state of calm, clarity, and well-being. Most importantly, I initiate a process for them to successfully have an alignment with the source within the center/authentic self and inner guidance system. In all of this, I wish to enable them to embrace their magnificence, get out of their own way, and deal with everyday challenges from a place of power and authority. I bring the transformational power of Holistic Spiritual and Metaphysical Life Coaching, Conscious Business/Mindful Leadership Coaching, Cognitive Behavior Therapy

Coaching, NLP (Neuro-linguistic programming) Coaching, EFT (Emotional Freedom Technique) Sessions, Customized Guided Meditation Sessions, and Mindfulness Workshops to private individuals, corporate organizations, and schools.

Acknowledgment

You were the most forgiving, kind, loving and generous person I know... Love you and miss you today and everyday Papa ✞ 🕯️

I thank my Dad for teaching us how to be kind, gentle, and good human beings, and encouraging us to dream big, treat others well, and have high self-worth. My Dad was so proud of us. He always made sure that everyone in the family loved, honored, and cared for each other. His deteriorating health in the last couple of years of his life pushed me deeper towards the higher power and this spiritual journey. Miss you, Papa!

I express deep gratitude to my Mom for sending me messages of blessings and best wishes every morning, sharing her spiritual study material with me, inspiring me, believing in me, and motivating me to exercise my potential to the maximum.

Ma (mother) a person in your life who will do anything for you just to bring a smile on your face, who will do anything for your happiness, and will never let you go to bed worried if she can help you take your worries away.

I can't wait to see the look on your face when you receive the first copy of my book. ☺

I thank my Husband Rajiv, and Son Rohit, for their constant love and support, which is the ultimate nectar of my life that keeps me going. Thanks, Rajiv, for all the ways you have contributed to my growth. Thanks, Rohit, for being My Coach whenever I needed one. ☺

I thank my elder brother Vibhu Ranjan for always encouraging and believing in me, telling me over and over that I am destined for greater achievements, and for reminding me the million ways he feels proud of having me as his little sister. I am forever grateful for your fatherly love.

I thank my elder sister Bhavana, for the enlightening conversations and constant inspiration through her own spiritual journey as a healer, her accomplishments, determination, and strength to overcome difficulties, teaching me that nothing is impossible. Thanks, Didi.

I thank my younger brother Varun for his unconditional love, support, and the motivation to actually start writing this book. This book will still be in my 'To Do' list if you had not propelled me to begin composing. Thanks, brother, for always being there for me.

Preface

"Do not strain yourself to understand all of life's mysteries at once. Accept each one as it comes and fit it into the jigsaw puzzle, knowing that bit by bit each piece will be shown to you and will fit into place perfectly. Become like an empty vessel ready to be filled."

-Eileen Caddy

Spiritual coaching is a process of discovering yourself, learning to accept your true spiritual essence and consciously create your world instead of reacting to outside influences. This book is the fruit of my journey and experience in the field.

Through this book, I have tried to reach out to my readers and help them connect to who they truly are. Hopefully this book will help you to change/explore or navigate your life, reveal your deepest desires and take the required actions to connect with your spiritual being. This book takes a more holistic approach and helps you tap into your inner consciousness and find that connection with the Divine.

As you read through the book and accompany me on this journey you will be able to assess and re-program your unconscious patterns to accomplish new and healthy ones. And once you master the art of unlearning and learning you will automatically find yourself dwelling in the good parts of yourself.

By the end of this book, you will be able to purge, release, and remove yourself from that which no longer serves your purpose. The more we understand our real nature, the fewer impediments we have in our lifetime. Spirituality and meditation go hand in hand. Spiritual knowledge and meditation when practiced together reveal benefits that one can only imagine of.

This book will show that spending some quiet time alone adjusts oneself to their inner world, harmony, and peace. Your feeling of self will extend as you experience life as a spiritual being appreciating humanity. You'll reach your comprehension of what your life and the Universe are tied in with. You'll go beyond the disorder and turmoil to a condition of harmony and happiness.

Readers will be able to realize that spirituality is pretty straightforward and practical, as well as it can be easily adapted in our everyday life.

Contents

Page Left Blank Intentionally

Chapter 1
Introduction

"We are all stars wrapped up in the skin, the light you are seeking has always been within."

We are spiritual beings having human experiences. Life is not just about waking up every day, repeating the same routine, working at the same place, and then dying one day, leaving everything behind you have invested your blood and sweat in. The crux of a healthy lifestyle lies beneath the thick layer of self-discovery and self-actualization.

People are so blinded by the worldly pleasures that they spend their whole lives chasing materialistic stuff. They lose themselves in the race of achieving nothing but short-term happiness. To reconcile with inner happiness, we must believe in the true power of connection and magic of spiritual unfoldment. Throughout our journey in this book, you will find chunks of yourself, and together we will try to trace back to the inner peace and happiness by joining those missing pieces.

Our self-belief and confidence are negatively affected by what we deem as a failure. The increasing rate of depression and other mental illnesses is because people are finding happiness, not within themselves, but outside, relying more on worldly stuff as a source of satisfaction, happiness, and joy.

As Ernesto Cardenal said, *"We turn outward, attracted by the beauty we see in the created things without realizing that they are the only reflection of the real beauty. And the real beauty is within us."*

My name is Vibha Sharma. I am a Holistic Spiritual and Metaphysical Life Coach, Mindful Leadership, and Conscious Business Coach.

My professional career revolves around the spiritual teachings, the field of meditation/mindfulness, and metaphysical laws. I facilitate a process for my clients to help them realize that there is 'something bigger' working behind the scenes, a golden thread, a force that binds everything together. Help from the higher power is always available. We are never alone.

Stepping into your divine identity helps you live a more peaceful, blissful life even among the outer chaos. Your outer problems seem less real, and solutions start flowing to you as 'goodies' just by being in touch with your 'real self.'

Everything starts fitting into the puzzle magically.

There is nothing to alter but our notion of self. As soon as we accomplish in changing ourselves, our world will disband and reconstruct itself in coherence and well-being.

Self-actualization is the key that opens many doors of wisdom and knowledge in different dimensions by broadening our horizons of thinking capability and the way we perceive life.

Born and brought up in India, I always had a strong connection with spirituality, religion, and matters of unworldliness. Since childhood, I was well aware of the existence of divine forces guiding and protecting us. I was raised in a family where we were exposed to a well-balanced lifestyle, comprising of equally religious and spiritual practices.

I saw my parents reading spiritual books and attending spiritual discourses, lectures, and gatherings. My Mom used to tell us Mythological stories from Hindu scriptures at night, and thus, I was introduced to a deeper side of life in my early childhood. With all those childhood experiences and memories which I experienced in typical Indian culture, I bring with me the sense of devotion, commitment, and faith because they are the essential ingredients of every self-awareness journey.

I have been an avid reader of self-help and spiritual books since childhood, and they have undoubtedly shaped who I am today. I was always intrigued by the idea of our spiritual connection, origin, and enlightenment. My whole life, I have been fascinated with metaphysics, the practice of mind expansion, meditation, and the law of attraction.

I first came to the US in late 1994 with my husband, immediately after getting married in India. I was fascinated with the natural beauty of California, its coasts, beaches, hills, and mountains, and very soon, I fell in love with this place.

Who knew at that time that this would prove to be the beginning of my spiritual journey and that I would grow as a source of providing comfort to other people at a professional level? I'm glad that it happened. America is a vibrant and beautiful country. There is a lot of cultural diversity. You have to feel it, experience it, and cherish it. The feeling may not be the same for some Indians since it is a relatively young civilization. However, the beauty of American culture to me is how accepting it is and the freedom it gives you.

I was still missing my parents and family back home while getting adjusted to a new way of life. After living a life one could possibly imagine, and having a living standard that people can only dream of, something kept bothering me. Maybe that feeling of unsettlement and desire to discover was nature's way of modeling my thoughts and directing my energy into utilizing my time by adopting my previous hobby of reading. After a few years of settling in and having my son, I started reading books on spirituality, metaphysics, and law of attraction again.

My husband had differing views on my working outside of the house since I had to be there for my kid as well. And working 9 to 5 at this stage would just deprive me of the quality time I could spend with my child. Thus, I decided to help my husband in his software consulting business while taking care of my son. All the free time I get through my routine, I would spend it studying and exploring the depths of my spiritual knowledge. So much so that, after seeing all the stuff around me, my husband would often crack a joke saying, "Your Ph.D. is not finished yet?"

When my son started going to school, my interest in this area grew deeper since I was able to find some more time for myself. During that time, I found out about Nichiren Buddhism.

"Desire is God tapping at the door of your mind, trying to give you greater good."

-H. Emilie Cady

The primary practice of Nichiren Buddhists is humming, basically the chant 'Nam Myoho Renge Kyo,' which signifies 'I devote my life to the law itself." Chanters reprise this chant to dwell into the depth of the spiritual practice of the Lotus Sutra. The chant is executed in front of a scroll called the Gohonzon. The mantra is referred to as daimoku, or in honorific form, o-daimoku. The purpose of chanting daimoku is to attain perfect and complete awakening. It refers to the great power inherent in a human being's life, i.e., the state of Buddhahood.

A primary idea in the SGI is the "human revolution" — the notion that the internal transformation of a person will eventually lead to a positive outcome in one's situations and ultimately in society as a whole. I started attending Buddhist gatherings and weekly meetings to chant together. I made some new friends and loved chanting and studying with them.

Gohonzon

The purpose of any chanting is to quiet the mind chatter and feel centered. Although chanting itself is proper formal practice, for starters, it is to observe silence while sitting. The real journey starts when we practice sitting in silence for a longer period of time. One day while arranging my husband's closet, I found a small booklet of Master Ching Hai. I could not put the booklet down and read the whole thing all at once. It was so tempting to know how, through meditation, we can access different realms and dimensions and go back to our source. I wanted to experience everything that was described in the book.

The Supreme Master Ching Hai
The Key of Immediate Enlightenment

I started meditating one hour each morning and evening, following everything that was required to get initiated into the Quan Yin Method described in the booklet to follow the path. I finally got initiated after two years of practicing the prerequisites.

Quan Yin Method -- the meditation on Inner Light and Inner Sound. The Inner Light, the Light of God, is the same Light referred to in the word "enlightenment." The inner sound is the Word referred to in the Bible: "In the beginning was the Word, and the Word was God..." It is through the inner Light and Sound that we come to know God.

After studying and practicing, I found out that the Quan Yin Method was the exact same as Sant Mat teachings that I learned in India attending spiritual discourses with my Mom.

I realized I was happier than ever by adopting regular daily meditation and noticed many positive changes in myself. My overall outlook toward life changed to a more positive one. I started attending local meditation classes and began studying several courses on the topic. I would go to each and every meditation class that was available locally. I ordered and read every book on enlightenment that I came across.

I read 'Divine Romance,' 'Man's Eternal Quest,' and 'Autobiography of a Yogi' by Swami Paramahansa Yogananda. These are amazing books that explained the science of spirituality in an astonishing way. I got introduced to Kriya Yoga. Kriya Yoga is a primordial meditation method of energy and breath control or pranayama.

As per Yogananda, Kriya is the most effective method accessible to humans today for attaining the aim of yoga, and union with the divine. The aim of these easy yet extremely effective yoga methods is to teach you to deal openly with energy and consciousness, thus empowering you to revive your body with energy, to rouse the mind's infinite power, and to experience deepening mindfulness of the Divine in your life.

I found out about Self Realization Fellowship (SRF), which is a global religious organization with international headquarters in Los Angeles. I registered myself in three years of Self Realization fellowship course, which gives step-by-step directions in the yoga methods of meditation, attentiveness, and energization, comprising Kriya Yoga. The teachings were assembled under Paramahansa Yogananda's direction. In addition to his inclusive guidelines in meditation, the course offered practical teachings for every aspect of spiritual living, how to live ecstatically, and fruitfully amidst the unending challenges and prospects in this changing world. This course prepares you for Kriya Yoga initiation.

I heard about a local Kriya Yoga initiation event, and after attending the event for two days, I got initiated into Kriya Yoga. It was a beautiful experience, and I made new like-minded friends at the event as well.

We used to have a Kriya Yoga meditation every weekend at a local assigned member's house for practice and advancement. It was such a good experience to be able to meditate with advanced members and fellow students.

At Ananda Palo Alto, CA

After getting initiated into the Quin Yin method (Similar to Sant-Mat) and Kriya Yoga, I realized how both the methods led us to the inner journey towards our source. I was attending Kriya Yoga classes every weekend and meditated twice a day, morning, and evening. I saw positive changes in myself and felt a great strength inside of me to deal with life's challenges, which are a part of everybody's life. The results of daily meditation astounded me, and I introduced this life-changing practice to my 8-year-old son. He was very receptive. I noticed calming effects on him and realized that it's extremely important to teach kids meditation at an early age. I took a few courses and read several books on 'Teaching meditation to kids' and started offering meditation classes to kids as well.

I became a spiritual seeker, dedicated to understanding mysteries of life. I took up meditation, read several books, attended classes, workshops, and went to spiritual gatherings whenever I got a chance to deepen my connection to the Divine.

Meditation and spiritual practice became a central part of my life, along with prayer, reading, and contemplation. Over the years, I read several books on spirituality and metaphysics by different philosophers such as teachings of Neville Goddard, Joel Goldsmith, Rev Ike, Esther Hicks, Andrew Murray, Emmet Fox, ACIM, Neal Donald Walsh, Rhonda Byrne, Gregg Braden, Eckhart Tolle, Wayne Dyer, Louise Hay, Emilie Cady, Lillian Dewaters, Michael Talbot, I AM discourses and Hindu philosophers such as Ramana Maharshi, Swami Paramahansa Yogananda, Nisargadatta, Hindu/Vedic and Sant Mat teachings.

My father's illness and the transition was a tough time for me. Being far, I was sad and worried about him all the time. I could not spend much time with him when he needed all of his children near him. This guilt kept me in a distressful and sad place for a long time. It made me realize that we are never prepared enough to deal with the loss, pain, and grief that follows. I am tearing up writing this as I can still hear him sometimes asking me 'Beta kab aayoge? I am waiting for you' (I am waiting for you dear, when will you come to visit us?) The practice of meditation and prayer gave me hope, strength, and peace to deal with the situation. I managed to stay balanced and brought myself out of that sorrowful state only because of my spiritual practice, study, and meditation. I realized that guilt is a universal symptom, common and normal emotion in grief, and we need to develop strength and find ways to accept, integrate, and move forward with these feelings.

The fear of losing loved ones was the greatest reason for me to pursue this path. I wanted to become immune to the pain by becoming enlightened and knowing the truth behind the veil.

Adapting meditation and developing my relationship with my source helped me understand that we are always connected with our loved ones. I remind myself of my place in eternity and our own limited time in this body.

It helped me stay true to myself and provided me the strength to cope up with external factors. I started to look beyond mere realities and became more aware of what lies beyond everybody's actions and life situations. Before the spiritual growth, I was too sensitive and used to feel miserable because of other people's insensitivity and behavior sometimes. But now all I need is my time, some quiet moments alone, and I am good to go. Instead of feeling disappointed over things that life brings sometimes, I pick up myself quickly by remembering the bigger picture and reminding myself that I am the master of my feelings. My happiness is not anybody's responsibility. Some people spend their whole lives quantifying and analyzing their life judgments. Their lives revolve around finding faults in others and justifying their own wrongdoings. Not even for once do these people bother to look within and try to correct themselves. If they did, they would be able to see their own negative perception and good in others. Self-analysis is the best type of individual growth.

"When you are spiritually connected, you are not looking for occasions to be offended, and you are not judging and labeling others. You are in a state of grace in which you know you are connected to God and thus free from the effects of anyone or anything external to yourself."
–Wayne Dyer

I have my clients come to me all the time and tell me how somebody's behavior at work or their personal life is causing them stress to the degree that it affects their self-esteem and peace of mind. We need to realize that when people judge hurt, blame, or criticize you, they only do it according to their inner state and level of consciousness. Their wounded self finds comfort in hurting others and that has nothing to do with you. The lack of love and security in their life spills outside. In such a scenario, we need to step into our own power and always remember that no outside force can change our mindset or our beliefs, only we can. It's better to withdraw ourselves from people who are not willing to change in order to protect our own peace.

The reality is that we can't completely block out the negative people but can always change the ratio in which we interact with them and, most importantly, the way we perceive and deal with the hostile people and situations.

Distance yourself from negativity, stay connected to your true self. 'Turn Within!'

I meditate twice daily, not that I am supposed to, but because I want to; it makes me feel so relaxed and peaceful. It has helped me evolve and attain higher levels of peace and inner satisfaction.

One of the reflective benefits I received through meditation that has made a great impact on my life is mindfulness of my state of being. The more I contemplate, the more I'm able to witness my opinions and reactions in my most judgmental, basic, disturbed, and non-meditating hours. This permits me to address my considerations and get a few perspectives in almost any circumstance I am in. I have gotten to be increasingly self-aware.

My day starts with contemplating, reading, and meditating. After waking up, I spend some quiet time alone to align myself with my inner world.

My consistent practice to connect to the Divine every day and all day long has not only helped me conquer all the challenges in my life, but it has given me a sense of purpose and has added meaning to my life.

"Even if you achieve your outer purpose, it will never satisfy you if you haven't found your inner purpose, which is awakening, being present, being in alignment with life. True power comes out of the presence; it is the presence."
-Eckhart Tolle

My ultimate trust in the ever-present spiritual assistance has always helped me overcome any difficulty I have ever faced in my life.

I have realized that every situation and everybody in our lives is placed according to the perfect divine plan. Everybody contributes and behaves according to his/her part assigned for our growth and divine destiny.

Each and every major phase of life from the early age of childhood to the teenage and to adolescence constitutes opening a new door of life. Stepping into the new phase is all about learning and adapting to deal with the demands and different challenges in a whole new way.

During all these years, I have studied and practiced several spiritual modalities for a single reason – to develop and become a better version of myself every day.

One day it occurred to me that if it's the last day of my life, how would I want to feel, how did I spend my life? What did I do with my life? And the answer was that I want to share with others what I learned and what I truly believe in. I realized that if there are a few things I can do all day long and feel fulfilled through, they are studying, practicing, and sharing the knowledge I have acquired over the years regarding spiritual teachings and their application to help them solve all kinds of problems.

I remembered how on multiple occasions, several people told me that a small casual conversation with me inspired them to make important changes in their lives, write a book or change the perspective about a situation they were facing at that time. I was speaking through my experiences and my knowledge, which built up as a mutual platform for people to relate and share. It made me notice how effortlessly I have been inspiring and motivating my family and friends all through my life. Being the middle child, I was a natural peacemaker in my family. I had this very basic instinct to calm situations and people down. This is one of the reasons that provoked my thinking to become a full-time holistic coach and help people through my knowledge and skill.

I completed several courses and certifications on Life Coaching, Meditation, Reiki, NLP (Neuro-linguistic programming, Cognitive Behavior Therapy (CBT), EFT (Emotional Freedom Technique), and a Certification in Conscious Business Coaching to equip myself to be able to coach different type of clients. I started working with people of all ages, kids, women, seniors, and professionals.

As a holistic spiritual life coach, its fulfilling to see the clients having breakthroughs and getting solid results by changing the way they function on a deeper level. We work together to create a customized action plan that helps my clients make positive life changes and move forward with confidence. Rather than just evaluating their behaviors, habits, and goals, I delve into their deep-rooted beliefs and their connection to the Divine. Several times, in just a single session, my clients see themselves in a whole new light and the way they were perceiving and contributing to a particular situation with their own limited view, that was bothering them for months. What happens? Nothing changes outside, but they do from inside.

I have noticed that deep down within, we all are aware of our truth, but sometimes we need somebody else to remind us what we have forgotten.

Each aspect of our life can impact others. Stressful situations in our lives can develop into physical manifestations. High levels of anxiety from a job or relationship can lead to low energy, poor nutrition, overeating, or even illness.

If you are feeling generally unfulfilled, this can create negative thinking patterns that could cause your emotional life to suffer. In my own experience and work with the clients, I have observed mindfulness as an extremely effective means of improving overall happiness and well-being.

The research accompanied by extensive practice with separate spiritual modalities and the knowledge I have attained by studying eastern and western philosophy enabled me to gain an insight into different perspectives of life to guide others seeking help. It helps me connect with people on a personal level and relate with them, irrespective of their beliefs, cultural backgrounds, and goals. It's gratifying to see that I spark a change in their lives with the aid of self-actualization, meditation, and mindfulness. My practice and teachings don't belong to a certain belief system. They are not a part of any religion or creed, but they do resonate with the followers of different spiritual systems.

"We keep moving forward, opening new doors, and doing new things, because we're curious and curiosity keeps leading us down new paths."

-Walt Disney

The reason I am writing this book is that I want to help the audience know the importance of their connection to the higher power within to overcome difficulties and live their life with purpose and clarity. I believe, within every problem lies the solution and the answer to our every query.

The whole notion behind naming the book 'Turn Within' is to imply that the only way out is the way in; there is a door inside. By walking into that door, you see a way to everything out. This journey of self-discovery is possible through a holistic approach towards life and seeking solutions for your day-to-day concerns. This book will serve the purpose of spreading awareness regarding meditation and the importance of connecting from within. We need to trace our lives back to our heavenly source to get to know the true essence of being alive. With the help of this book, I will try to convey my teachings and findings to the readers based on my personal, professional, and social experiences. Most people will adopt the holistic way of life, but they don't know in which direction they should take the first step.

This book will give them a push start by providing them some spiritual principles, teachings, and techniques to grow and develop their mind. Most of the people who have had no experiences of spirituality (staying centered within), find it difficult, which is obviously not the case. With the aid of my writing, they will be able to realize that spirituality is actually pretty easy and practical, and it can be easily adapted in our everyday life.

"You do not need to leave your room. Remain sitting at your table and listen. Do not even listen, simply wait, be quiet, still, and solitary. The world will freely offer itself to you to be unmasked, it has no choice, and it will roll in ecstasy at your feet."

–Franz Kafka

Chapter 2
Spirituality Holds the Answer

Devarayanadurga Temple, Karnataka, India

"Everything is laid out for you. Your path is straight ahead of you. Sometimes it's invisible, but it's there. You may not know where it's going, but you have to follow that path. It's the path to the Creator. It's the only path there is."
-Chief Leon Shenandoah

The constant struggle, the constant search for happiness, and the constant thought of being empty from the inside despite having everything needed to live a happy and healthy life depict the unsettlement and lack of satisfaction or contentment. The answers to more happiness, peace, and greatness are not to be found in the goals you're chasing. You are the creator of your life but not in the way you've been conditioned to believe. You can live the life you dream about, not through working harder and for longer, but by reconnecting to the divine wisdom within and reclaiming the inner peace and joy through simple meditation practice and a firm belief in Divine. Spending thousands of dollars on fancy trips cannot guarantee peace at all.

"Though you may travel the world to find the beautiful, you must have it within you, or you will find it not."
–Ralph Waldo Emerson

We all know that when we are at peace internally, we are exposed to many physiological, psychological, and spiritual benefits. When your body is at rest, and your mind is at peace, your ability to concentrate enhances, and you are able to focus more clearly. This state of mind evokes a sense of inner strength and power, which gives birth to the feeling of self-confidence and breeds positivity, promising you an overall healthy lifestyle.

When we work on ourselves from within, we evolve into a new personality, something better than the previous one. Our new journey of life begins the day we realize our self-worth and discover our inner self. For sure, the human body is more than just flesh and bones and we realize its true value on our journey towards self-dependency, self-actualization, and the healing of mind and body through meditation.

Ancient sages have always emphasized that man's first duty is to know himself. The Greek Philosophers said:

"Worship the Gods, if you must; but your first duty is to find out who and what you are yourself." So, they wrote over the doors of their temples, "Gnothe Seauton"

-Know Thyself

One of the biggest delusions of this modern world is that happiness and satisfaction come from a higher rank, fame, or money. They can buy you temporary satisfaction in the name of happiness, but these are the weakest of all sources if you are looking for true happiness. If this were true, we wouldn't see celebrities attempting suicides.

"I think everybody should get rich and famous and do everything they ever dreamed of so they can see that it's not the answer."

-Jim Carrey

You cannot buy peace of mind or inner satisfaction through worldly stuff. For that, you need to work on yourself, evaluate your inner self, and realize your actual worth.

"It isn't enough to talk about peace. One must believe in it. And it isn't enough to believe in it. One must work at it."
-Eleanor Roosevelt

Every morning, when I spend some time alone to align myself with my inner world, I get "clear messages" to carry the idea to practice for the day. I have noticed as long as I remain aligned with the idea or practice, I feel very peaceful and calm. Sometimes a message from my reading material catches my eye, and I immediately take note of it. These notes help me significantly whenever I need clarity and direction. I collect them for easy access and use them with my clients. I am passionate about holistic life coaching and teaching people the art of meditation for leading a **peaceful and spirit-centered life.** Meditation teaches us how to fulfill our soul, how to feel completely satisfied from within ourselves, and how to be more emotionally stable. Sometimes in life, we experience trauma or incidents that take a heavy toll on us. Maybe you are going through that stage where everything seems like the end of the world, and you feel like you are falling into the deep dark pit of nothingness. Maybe you feel like there's no way out of this situation, and by every passing second, the feeling gets more intense.

Maybe you feel hollow from inside as if you are corroding slowly and gradually as if your fears are chasing the sanity of your mind and questioning your mental stability. It could be that you feel like you can never recover from this trauma, or even if you do, you won't be able to heal completely. Behold and turn within as this is the place you will find the cure to every sorrow. Open the inner door of inner peace and well-being and Be Transformed!

"Be still and know! Seek ye the kingdom of God, and everything else shall be added unto you!"

Every now and then, we hear of students and successful and famous people committing suicide. The other night we heard Lady Gaga talk about the importance of mental health in her 2019 Grammys acceptance speech. Last year, the suicides of Anthony Bourdain and Kate Spade stunned and saddened the world. People like them who are otherwise known as very successful in their lives, suffer silently for years, feeling empty and not enough. They must be in a really dark and lonely place to make such a decision to end their life.

I feel the need to educate people about the daily practice of meditation, stillness or centering, whatever you call it, but that which entails connecting with the inner spirit, higher power, divine order, or infinite creative power every single day. I feel I could have helped that person...that person could have given himself/herself another chance of finding and connecting themselves on the inside.

In spite of all the material success, sometimes people feel lost and miserable. It's not that we can judge their decision or their pain. If only they could see the light within, the peace, the eternal well-being, and the truth. If only they realize that every life has a purpose. If only they express their soul's mission of helping others, they will never take such a step. When we make an effort to express ourselves in a noble way, we never feel depressed. Why do people decide to end their life when they can connect to the inner fountain of peace and bliss and transform their lives and that of people around them?

"Celebrities can suffer horrible loneliness even though they have millions of fans. I started doing meditations because I realized that a spiritual path was necessary".

-Donovan

God has sent every individual on earth with some purpose, no matter what your story is, and how different you think it is from other people's life. Every event that has happened to you was to shape you and to strengthen you more than before. Every situation, either good or bad, serves a purpose in your life. Even in bad situations, we need to stay resilient and extract the best out of them. God will not put you through anything you cannot handle. You are stronger than you think.

All you need to do is recognize your strength and unique qualities that God Almighty has bestowed upon you. He has equipped every creation, every individual with unique qualities and capabilities, which no one can ever possibly replace. There is a Divine plan and a purpose, a value to every life, regardless of the location, age, gender, ability, or disparity. Find the lesson and purpose in the darkest events of your life, boldly facing whatever may come your way, making sure you are never a victim of your circumstances but a victor. Use your mind as your friend that tells you that you can do all things through the power of God, the power of your divinity. Don't let your mind become your own enemy that finds happiness in your defeat and doesn't want you to succeed. A mind telling you that you are a victim will leave you hopeless, because if you fall for it, then you cannot achieve anything, and ultimately, you will not be able to overcome the negative situations in your life.

Connect yourself with that divine power on a daily basis. It should be the first thing in the morning you do and the last thing before you sleep. When you are aligned and connected with the power inside you, you have his protection and guidance all the time. **Turn Within!**

"God is not revealed through outward observation but through inward experience. If a revelation is requested by a person, then it cannot be received since the act of asking is a statement that is not there. Such a statement produces the experience of not having. Our thoughts are creative, and

our words are productive. Thoughts and words give birth to reality."

-Neale Donald Walsch

When we look for outer validation for our happiness, we feel sad. We can be the kindest, nicest person, but for some people, we will never be enough. No matter what we do, they will always find something wrong in our behavior. Instead of feeling disappointed, we need to remind ourselves that whatever people see depends on their consciousness, their own inner reality, their inner perception, and it has nothing to do with us.

Lord Jesus said, *"ye shall know the truth and truth shall make u free."*

Often times, people have amazing lives with fulfilling rewards. They may have an active social life, fame, wealth, progressing professional development, but what they lack is the fulfillment, peace, and joy. Inner satisfaction cannot be bought materialistically. In order to be able to discover the peace that your mind and soul are craving for, you need to turn within. People often mistake their yearning for peace and inner satisfaction with worldly pleasures and try to compensate for the empty void with materialism. They rely on objects and other people for the sake of their own happiness, whereas true happiness comes from within.

Being distant from the Creator leads to people wandering in search of inner peace. The sense of separation from our Creator is the root cause of all the miseries that we experience. When we are disconnected from our spirit self, we experience a lack of joy and peace and just don't feel good from the inside. We try to find reasons to justify such feelings. However, this is never the case. The only reason we feel empty is our disconnection or deviation from our source. The outer world will always change, as inconsistency is the most consistent thing!

The safety or security you find in the physical world is not everlasting, and all of it will be gone one day. When you're not at peace, it's a sure sign of your 'misalignment' and a weak connection with the Creator. The joy that you will feel after aligning yourself with the Creator is something that you will never get from any worldly thing.

As we are aligned and centered in our being, no matter what happens outside, we stay balanced and at peace, knowing the bigger picture and the meaning of all the situations in our life. The measure of ultimate success is always peace.

"Happiness, true happiness, is an inner quality. It is a state of mind. If your mind is at peace, you are happy. If your mind is at peace, but you have nothing else, you can be happy. If you have everything the world can give – pleasure, possessions, power – but lack peace of mind, you can never be happy."

-Dada Vaswani

Using alcohol or any substance as an escape is just another illusion that deceives your thinking, and by the time you realize it, it's too late to go back.

I see people being slaves to this nasty addiction, which, instead of helping them, eats them hollow from the inside. Even after years of drinking, you will find yourself standing at the exact same point where you were years ago. Nothing will change except for your mental and physical health, which will have worsened already.

Once Rumi said, "the wound is where the light enters the body." It signifies that a person's ability of resilience is what defines his or her character. Nobody's life is perfect or turns out as they plan it to be, there's no definition to living a perfect life, it is us who bring out the best in every situation which makes life beautiful. Every other person you see on the street is going through something you may not be aware of. Everybody is fighting their own battle, but the question is, how far are we into that battle? Do you see the light at the end of the tunnel, or are you just fighting every day from the moment you wake up to the very second you force yourself to sleep at night? Do you see any progress in your approach, or is it just a mere coping mechanism to survive another day of life?

Spirituality holds the answer to all these questions, and not just answers, but their cures as well. The first step to achieving spiritual healing is self-actualization, and knowing your actual worth. We spend our lives chasing the nothingness of worldly materials. There is nothing wrong in aspiring for material success, but being discontent and too attached to worldly possessions leaves us feeling powerless and empty.

"When you are discontent, you always want more, more, more. Your desire can never be satisfied. But when you practice contentment, you can say to yourself, 'Oh yes – I already have everything that I really need."

-Dalai Lama

Let go of whatever has happened in the past. Take your past as a source of learning from failure or bad experiences, and remember the joy you felt during your happy times, as those are the moments you should cherish throughout your life. Your past does not define you. What defines you is your conduct toward life and how you take the events of the past into shaping your future.

Start fresh, start strong, and connect yourself with your source. You will find your own purpose and strength, and once you are aware of your own power, every day will be a new day for you. Recognize your divinity, and witness how you'll live a totally different life.

We are eternal, we were always there, and we will always be. We cannot just evaporate into nothingness. We have to come to this material plane until we fulfill our purposes assigned by the Almighty. We will keep facing the challenges we need to learn our lessons from.

Everybody has a limited time on this earth, we have to leave this body one day, so why not do our best to make our lives worthwhile and meaningful as much as we can? You are never too late to take the first step in becoming a better version of yourself. It is always the first step that requires the most courage, and after that, you just have to follow the pattern and go with the flow. Once you are aware of your potential, power, and capability, you will start each day with a goal, hope, and a positive mindset to achieve something new, leaving behind all your sorrows and the things which used to haunt your dreams.

> *"If you cannot find peace within yourself, you will never find it anywhere else."*
> **-Marvin Gaye**

My father always used to tell us that our relationship with God is as of a small child with his or her father. When a kid goes to a fair holding his father's hand, he goes here and there, enjoys the true colors, games, rides, and the crowd. The sense of protection and fearlessness motivates the kid to explore more and more. He is not scared of anyone because he knows his father is there with him, his protector, his shield against any danger, or anything that is harmful.

Imagine how he would feel if he gets separated from his father in the middle of the crowd? The same scenario, the same surroundings will completely turn the opposite for him. He will feel more exposed and vulnerable to threats and dangers. Everything around him will be the same, and nothing would have changed. He would still be standing there in the middle of the same crowd, but all the attractions, colors, games, and lights would not seem exciting to him anymore. He would cry, feeling scared, insecure, and vulnerable. The feeling of fear will haunt him – of being lost in the crowd and never returning home. Our connection with our Creator lies on the same principles. We will go astray, wandering in the dark if we leave His hand. Establishing a relationship with our heavenly father will not only let us enjoy the worldly pleasures more, but will give us an inner assurance that our Lord, our Savior, has our back. We will feel secure and protected by all the evils and the worldly harm. When we are self-assured, we can face anything life throws at us. If any difficulty or challenge arises, we will be aware that we are not fighting alone, and that God is always with us.

"Truth has rushed to meet you since you called upon it. If you knew Who walks beside you on the path that you have chosen, fear would be impossible."

-ACIM

Once you connect yourself to God/the Higher Power, you will find new strengths, protection, and guidance every single day. Not only will you be able to take care of yourself better, but you will also be a source of strength and help to others – a beacon of hope and guidance. No matter how different or bad your situation is, another person could be going through something far worse. Everybody has his/her own battle to fight. Helping others has a significant positive impact on our minds. It evokes a sense of fulfillment, a sense of self-growth, and eternal happiness.

"God has given us two hands. One to receive with and the other to give with."
-Billy Graham

Every kind gesture can have an impact on someone's day, even if it is just passing a smile. We have become so tangled up in our everyday lives that these expressions seem to be fading away from our everyday socializing. We laugh only with the people we want to, and we help the only people we want to, which is wrong. Kindness shouldn't be shown to certain people only.

Helping a blind person cross the street, helping an old person carry his/her load, letting somebody go first in the waiting line, are the small acts of kindness which may look small and don't require a lot of your time but have a significant impact on other people's lives.

Growing up in an Indian household, we would have very frequent visits from guests – mostly unexpected. But never even for once in life, I saw my mother complaining or my dad frowning. Instead, they would look out for opportunities to be able to help others. My father, although not super-rich, was a very generous man and had a heart of gold. He would welcome everyone with a big smile on his face.

Even if you think you have nothing to help others with, there is always something you can do for others. Just decide you can and you will see yourself supported in several ways. When you spread happiness, it comes back ten folds. This life is a blessing despite the challenges and difficult situations you may have faced in the past.

Every person is doing exactly what he/she needs to do in order to fulfill the divine plan of their lives. You meet people for a reason. You don't just run into people in your life for no reason. Each one of them serves a distinctive purpose, helps us grow, and become better versions of ourselves.

People who make us feel miserable are the biggest learning sources in our lives as they provide us experiences which we cannot get from any institution. These experiences help us learn and avoid repeating the same mistakes.

Everybody is just helping us in one way or another, then why not be at the better side of life and serve as a source of happiness and comfort to someone? We just need to find the higher purpose and message behind every situation by connecting ourselves to our source more often.

"We're all just walking each other home."
-Ram Dass

Chapter 3
Spiritual Quest

"The important thing is not to stop questioning. Curiosity has its own reason for existence. One cannot help but be in awe when he contemplates the mysteries of eternity, of life, of the marvelous structure of reality. It is enough if one tries merely to comprehend a little of this mystery each day".

-Albert Einstein

As the famous saying goes, what you seek is seeking you, it evokes our senses that this world is a continuous process of a series of events occurring in chronological order. You are destined to be where you are; however, the quest to work hard for it should never come to a halt. Who knows if destiny requires you to work for it in order to achieve it. You need to listen to your inner self and turn within. There are times when a person finds himself or herself alone, stranded, and no one to turn to. That is the time you need to listen the most to your true self, listen to the silence, what solitude has to say to you, to the still small voice.

As Joel Goldsmith glorifies its true meaning, the purpose of *The Infinite Way* is to cultivate spiritual awareness, not mainly to yield health out of sickness or wealth out of lack. Those are the additional benefits, and those who attain even a grain of spiritual insight are showing forth health, affluence, and happiness, and thus living their lives better than before and better than anyone.

This is not an objective, however. The goal is to achieve the spiritual revelation so that we can observe God's universe and can harmonize with Him, walk and talk with Him, live with Him, and learn to live with one another, and not just humanly because our blissful human companionships are much more worthwhile when we have achieved an amount of spiritual companionship.

The enlargement of spiritual awareness is the highest accomplishment there is. Only in the amount of this attained awareness are we able to witness the spiritual forms of God's creation. This has nothing to do with the growth of the mind or with any intellectual powers; as a matter of fact, it is not about accomplishing the feeling of knowing more than we knew before. It is a matter of attaining a profundity of inner consciousness, an awareness that articulates itself not so much in words as in feelings.

We cannot embrace new ideas while still adhering to the obsolete beliefs of the past: we must be willing to surrender our old notions. That is where courage comes in. It takes courage to leave behind what has proved to be inadequate in our experience.

The development of spiritual consciousness begins with our initial realization that what we are beholding through the senses of sight, hearing, taste, touch, and smell is not the reality of things. The first ray of spiritual illumination brings us hints of the divine, eternal, and immortal, which enables us to behold more and more of Reality. Because the human scene is entirely a misconception through misperception, any thought of helping, healing, correcting, or changing the material picture must be relinquished so that we may see the ever-present Reality.

Spirituality or having a spiritual connection is significantly important in one's life, shapes its conduct, as well as serves as a coping mechanism in difficult situations in life. When things get difficult, and you see no way out, behold! There is a lot that you are yet unaware of. When you find your beliefs different from what your common sense is telling you, maybe you just need to view the situation from another approach. This is more effective than adhering to controlling ideas that get in your way.

In order to Heal, you need to Connect!

Spirituality is not withdrawing into a state of diminution, but it is more about conceding to the longing pain and suffering and then ruling a way to mold that into the source of love and light. Spirituality is all about giving in to the celestial source and letting it purge out the hate from our minds that is blocking the passage for the spiritual enlightenment to penetrate through those thick membranes of the brain and heart. When we are hurt or lost, we recoil into our sadness, which further adds to our destruction. It affects not just our mental health severely but is also reflected through our physical appearance as we fail to perform appropriately in our everyday lives.

"He heals the brokenhearted and binds up their wounds."
-Psalms 147:3

To heal is to recover, to be at peace, to fight the inner demons that are holding you back from moving further in life – to heal is to set one's soul and mind at peace. Healing is something that cannot be achieved in an instant or overnight. You have to go through a process, or sometimes a series of multiple processes to reach that state of mind where you are no longer bothered by what used to haunt you.

In order to heal, you need to stand tall in front of your fears, look them in the eyes, that you are not afraid of them anymore, and witness how you no longer will feel suppressed. In order to heal, we need to break the chains of decades-old cruelty, silence, fear, oppression, loneliness, and come out clean to the brighter side of life. The journey to healing is tough but not impossible.

Don't let your stored emotions burst out into some kind of retaliation or anger; neither let it corrode your body and soul from the inside. Don't live with your fears. Value the life that God has granted you, and try to make the most of it by making it better every day. Just don't give up on yourself and believe in the magic of love – **loving your own self**, as this is the quickest and most effective method of healing.

When you love yourself, you won't let anything harm your aura. When your mind is at peace, you are more productive and are able to draw better conclusions or decisions. When your body is at rest and your mind is not dealing with any delusional thoughts, your energy is directed toward finding solutions rather than thinking about the troubles, troubles that aren't even there yet – in other words, anxiety.

Connecting to the Divine is a simple course that entails the strengthening of spiritual vibration to align with the vibration of the Divine. You don't necessarily need to move to remote places to find that spiritual enlightenment; just give yourself the chance to grow and to nurture in everyday life.

"Worldly people go outward, but you must go inward like the turtle, withdrawing within your shell."
-Neem Karoli Baba

We are all led by the power of our thinking; whatever we perceive, we begin to believe. Our mind is a powerful weapon against all the odds. Once you start meditating, you will notice miraculous changes to your mind and body, as if the nerves that have been blocked for ages are reopening. Use your mind to channel all your negativity into the possibility of achieving the positive goals no matter what the circumstances are. Once you have convinced your mind and yourself that no problem is as big as it may seem, you can fight through it

We are all fighting our inner demons. Offer others around you the liberty to grow. Evacuate any kind of controlling conduct. Individuals around us are fighting their own tough battles. They keep on striding on alone, without looking for help. Instead of becoming hindrances in their path, we should encourage them to emerge victorious from the battles they are fighting mentally.

"Be kind, for everyone you meet is fighting a battle you know nothing about."
-Wendy Mass, The Candymakers

Take baby steps every day towards the positive side of life; don't go harsh on yourself with a coarse routine. Evaluate yourself every day before you go to bed and identify what you have achieved so far. Our Physical health goes beyond the means of the physical body. It is more about what we give and receive. Health is also about our emotions and how we are feeling spiritually as well as mentally. With all these hectic routines and busy schedules, we often forget to spare some time for ourselves. We get so busy with our commitments, with work, family, and our social circle, that we hardly pay attention to the details that have a direct impact on our health. Developing a positive mindset will help you in many ways, more than you can think of.

Moreover, once you learn how to stay happy and positive, you will experience a new sense of wave around you, as if your aura is emitting rays of energy and happiness, resulting in the release of endorphins. This eventually boosts your confidence, therefore making you capable of taking more new challenges and working outside of your comfort zone. Training your brain to groom and seeing the positive in everything is a healthy sign that your brain is evolving and making more space for mental growth and happiness.

Negative thinking refers to the pattern your brain operates in. This can result in various severe mental health issues such as depression, anxiety, schizophrenia, personality disorders, and such. Furthermore, a negative mindset can highly affect the way you work, study, and carry out your social life as well. The problem with a negative mindset is that whenever your brain registers a negative thought, it narrows down your thinking ability by restricting your vision in one dimension.

Chronic negative thinking that goes day after day and eventually multiplies creates stress on your brain and nerves that can have a significant impact on your physical and mental health. However, our mind has a secret defense mechanism to protect our brain from reacting to all those negative emotions, which lead to depression. But it's like justifying a wrong thing with an equally wrong thing since depression is, of course, lethal for us. It threatens the survival of the body due to stress.

Therefore, we can draw a conclusion from this that a negative mindset creates troubles for you that were not even there in the first place. It makes you overthink every single thought by narrowing down your thinking approach toward every problem. Now it is in our hands how we direct our thinking and energy. One of the biggest factors contributing to a better, prosperous, healthy lifestyle is the maintenance of a healthy state of mind. If you have a positive mindset, it will accumulate all of your mind's space, thereby leaving no room for negativity. This signifies that you are either positive or negative; no one can dwell between both states of mind. How energies, either good or bad, can affect an individual's aura is explained in the research carried out by a Japanese researcher, Dr. Masaru Emoto. He proposed a theory after carrying out an experiment by highlighting the phenomenon of 'Hado,' meaning wave and move.

He described the effect of bad vibrations reflecting on the structure and changes in the pattern of water droplets by experimenting with two separate water jars. He exposed both the specimens to different surroundings and kept them under different circumstances. The reason he chose water is that most of the human body is made up of water, thus causing the same effect on the human body.

What Emoto basically wanted to do with this experiment was to keep them both under the opposite circumstances and notice any apparent changes. In order to achieve his desired results, he took this one jar of water and played rock music near it, signifying that rock music had a negative effect on the liquid contained in the jar. On the contrary, he praised the other jar, referred to it as Mother Teresa, and even sang to it. Reaching toward the final stages of the experiment, what he did was that he took one drop from each jug and stored them in the refrigerator, thereby letting them freeze. Once the droplets were cooled down and frozen, he then took both of them under the eye of his magnifying glass in order to observe any behavioral changes in the freezing patterns. He was amazed by the results he obtained from his research. He wrote in his paper that one of the water droplets that came from the "positive jar" had the pattern as of a beautiful frozen fine crystal, while the one that came from the negative jar was all distorted, broken, and its color was off as well.

Another example we have from our everyday lives is that when we talk to our plants, we see them nurturing and growing. The change in their health and growth is visible and evident in their physical appearance. On the other hand, the same plants, if left alone, ignored, and not taken care of, die their own death. Every day we have thoughts ranging from strong emotions of negativity to questionability of our instincts. These thoughts are going to turn our bodies hollow.

They will corrode us from the inside by transforming every single thought to mental diseases that will gradually affect our physical health as well. It's just one of the laws of nature that, however you mold your thoughts, your body is going to adapt to those changes by affecting your health positively or negatively, as life is 25% what happens to us and 75% how we react and alter to the consequences.

Here, I would like to ask you these questions:

Do you secretly struggle with constant anxiety and unease because on paper you have a great life, yet internally you're not content?

Do you often feel empty inside? Do you have an active social life and still feel lonely inside?

Are you seeking something outside of yourself - going after bigger goals, chasing the next deal, and creating a state of busyness? When all this is really doing is filling the void, dulling your senses, and locking out peace?

Stress, depression, dissatisfaction all stem from a disconnection with your divine source, your life energy, and a loving Universe.

The sense of something missing that keeps you up at night is your guidance, indicating that now is your time to attune yourself to your powerful truth.

The truth is that when you are aligned with your spiritual self, you experience more peace, more clarity, and more happiness. And the deeper you go into your truth, as though rousing the sleeping giant, you awaken the potential that exists within you, to take your life to the next level.

Spend some quiet time alone every single day.

"The summit of Reality can only be realized within oneself"

-Buddha

Spirituality is not just a practice. It's a divine experience that takes us beyond human limitations. Through spiritual learning, we get to explore who we are and what our life is actually about. Spirituality is often referred to as an experience of getting in touch with your own honorable compass — a method of knowing what is right and what is wrong, rendering to your own beliefs and philosophies. These beliefs do not need to be passed to you by religion; you can learn them by discovering your own thoughts and spirit. The journey of self-discovery is often difficult but never impossible. I know how challenging it can be to bring a change to your life. With my clients, we carry out a step-by-step plan based on their beliefs and background, and it's always gratifying to see the results they get to live a joyful, passionate life they deserve to be living.

> *"It takes courage...to endure the sharp pains of self-discovery rather than choose to take the dull pain of unconsciousness that would last the rest of our lives."*
> **-Marianne Williamson, A Return to Love: Reflections on the Principles of "A Course in Miracles**

Chapter 4
Self-Development

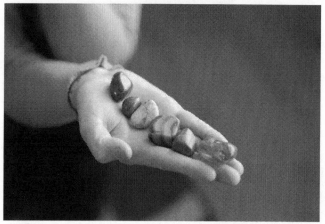

"Change your conception of yourself and you will automatically change the world in which you live. Do not try to change people; they are only messengers telling you who you are. Revalue yourself and they will confirm the change."
-Neville Goddard, Your Faith is Your Fortune

Do you feel like you're living life on the proverbial hamster wheel? Are you spinning your wheel fast but getting nowhere due to the constant stress of some professional, physical, or personal challenges? Do you have a nagging feeling of discomfort? We often feel lost on the track of life, confused and tangled within our own miseries. The thick mist of confusion around us clogs up our brain and arteries, preventing our thinking capability and the ability to make decisions. We continuously dwell between who we are and what we really want to be but never quite find the time to reflect upon our findings and answers.

Do you consider yourself to be very successful professionally, financially, and personally but still feel weighed down by a sense of powerlessness? As though you can't fully enjoy the fruits of your hard work because something is missing. Do you feel like there's a void within you that's obstructing your life goals?

Most people try to fill that void with an active social life, but does that actually prove to be fruitful? As discussed earlier, often, people seek refuge by getting indulged in activities such as alcoholism or drug abuse. People struggle to face life challenges, which have them turning to unhealthy habits and severe addictions to feel better or enjoy monetary pleasures. You are trying to heal, but the method you are opting for healing is going to lead you into further darkness. You are gradually pushing yourself into further depression. Sooner or later, you will become the victim of your own self-destructive behavior if not stopped right away. We are all victims of our own surroundings and what we are fed through them. Although deep down, you know that there's something more to life than just working hard, making a living, paying bills, and then dying one day. Due to our upbringing, we fall into the trap of believing that it is always supposed to be hard. All those challenges are part of life's rich tapestry.

You're seeking more peace, balance, and contentment in your life, but still, you question whether it's possible. Yes! It is indeed possible. The truth is that you deserve to live a peaceful, content life that you have always wished for. When you start understanding your true nature, you will notice a significant change in yourself, as well as in your surroundings. The only thing you need to do is to take the first step toward it.

All that we are is the result of what we have thought. If a man speaks or acts with an evil thought, pain follows him. If a man speaks or acts with a pure thought, happiness follows him, like a shadow that never leaves him.

-Gautama Buddha

We can live a fulfilling life by connecting ourselves to our divine source by cultivating a stronger relationship with our inner self.

When we align ourselves daily with that higher power - the force inside of us, our true Self– even if we have all the challenges outside, we still feel safe, protected, balanced, and at peace. This ultimately leads us to the solutions we could not see before. Things start flowing smoothly in our lives. Synchronicities take place.

Awareness Opens Gates into the New Realms

Self, Awareness, and Consciousness!

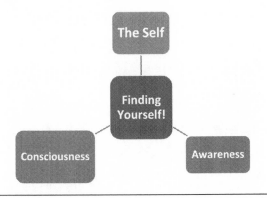

The Self

What is self to you? How do you define it in your own words? Let's look at the extract from the writings of Sri Ramana Maharishi – Be as you are!

"The Self that in which all these worlds seem to exist steadily, that of which all these worlds are a possession, that from which all these worlds rise, that for which all these exist, that by which all these worlds come into existence and that which is indeed all these - that alone is the existing reality. Let us cherish that Self, which is the reality, in the Heart"

-Sri Ramana Maharishi

The Difference between the Mind and the Self

Most people have a vague definition of the interrelation between the mind and the self. According to Ramana Maharishi, there is no variance between the mind and the self. The mind, if turned inwardly, is the self; if turned outwardly, it becomes the ego and all the world. He further explained that it is just like different clothes made out of cotton, but all of them named differently, and just like gold ornaments, all of them with a distinctive name and identity.

But in the end, they are all cotton and gold. The purity lies within the substance, which is gold; the one is real, and the rest of them are just mere names given to different byproducts. However, the mind does not exist without the self – it has no sovereign existence of its own. Whereas, the Self can exist without the mind. It has its own identity that is independent of any names attached to it.

What does a Man See upon Realizing the Self?

Sri Ramana Maharishi says, 'There is no seeing. Seeing is only being.'' The state of self-realization –as we call it – is not something to attain or achieve as in like a goal. Rather it is to be what you really are and what you have always been. All that is needed is that you give up your comprehension of the not-true as true. We are surrounded by the thick layer of confusion that we regard every unreal thing as real. All that we need to do is to give up this practice on our part that is blinding our vision to realize the Self, or as we say, "Be the Self."

In the quest to find the Self, there might come the point where you will doubt your decision in the first place; is it worth it? Or what am I doing? Well, it is pretty much normal to laugh at yourself when you are on a journey of discovering the self and becoming aware. That stage exceeds the seer and the seen. There is no seer there to see anything. The seer who is seeing all this now ceases to exist, and the Self alone remains.

Knowing the Self

If we talk about knowing the self, we need to realize that there are two self(s); the one that is known and the one that is unknown – hidden to the reality. The state of realization, as we refer to it as, is not to know anything or achieve anything; it is simply being oneself. You need to realize that you were born alone, and you stay that way until you die and even after that. The mere realization of this state can help you achieve new levels of spirituality. In addition to that, Sri Ramana claimed in the light of spiritual guidance and teaching practices that the state – the state of realization – cannot be described but only experienced. And of course, we casually talk a lot about the concept of self-realization – there are a number of books about it too – but it is because that is not actually what self-realization actually is. We name it that because we do not have any better term for it.

Furthermore, Sri Ramana described the intertwining relationship between the self and the silence. His message guides us that when a person is in absolute silence, he has only himself or herself. This, again, is linked to the idea of being born alone and dying alone – we are born with the self. The reason we need to seek it is that we are blinded by the worldly colors and lights; we have lost our SELF somewhere. For those who live in SELF as the beauty devoid of thought, there is nothing that should be thought of. That which should be adhered to is only the experience of silence because, in that supreme state, nothing exists to be attained other than oneself.

One known to the self
"Knowing the Self means being the Self."

One cannot claim that he or she does not know the Self. Though you cannot see it through your eyes, nor is it tangible to the senses, but can you deny the existence of your eyes? You cannot see your eyes, but you know they are there; you are aware of the self – although the self is not materialized or objectified. Even if you are not provided with a mirror, you can surely claim that you have your eyes.

Sri Ramana explains that when one says they cannot know the self, it is due to the lack in terms of relative knowledge. People are so accustomed to the relative knowledge that they identify and relate their selves with it. We are so indulged in materialism that we don't feel the existence of anything unless it is tangible or objectified. Such a wrong identity has forged the difficulty of not being able to see through situations and objects. We see what we are shown. We are blinded not to see beyond it. This materialism has blocked the possibility of knowing the obvious self because the self cannot be objectified. For one who has understood his Self, it is said that he will not have the three states of restlessness, dream, and deep sleep. Most of the people have this vagueness in their mind where they are unable to see through it. If a person says that he or she had a dream, or they were in a deep sleep, or they are awake, you must confess that they were there in all these three states.

He explained that a person is in all three states all the time. For instance, right now, you are awake, reading this, that means you are in the state of wakefulness, but that doesn't mean that you have excluded the other states from your system. In fact, when your wakefulness has been layered by your state of dream and sleep, just like it does when you are asleep or in dreams, your state of wakefulness is overshadowed.

This is just like a movie cinema with one singular screen but multiple screenings at different times. This means that you were there, you are there, and you will be there; now, at this moment, you are present in that state. The three states come and go as a rotational cycle, but you stay there. They appear on the screen and then vanish; nothing stays stuck to the screen.

Sri Ramana explains the atrocities and the ups and downs in the life of a human being with reference to knowing the self. If you convince yourself that you are there in all three states and they are not going to cause trouble for you anyhow, your life will be easier, and you will be better able to take challenges that life throws at you. He says that there are times when there is a picture of high-altitude waves of the ocean on the screen, and other times there is a great blazing fire, but does that affect the screen?

Does the picture of the waves wet the screen, or does the fire burn it? No! Why? Because the screen is not going anywhere, it is stood in it-SELF, it is the pictures and the scenarios appearing on it that keep on changing. In the same way, the things that transpire during the wakeful, dream and sleep states do not distress you at all; you endure your own Self.

Reaching the Self

"There is no reaching the Self. If SELF were to be reached, it would mean that the Self is not here and now and that it is yet to be obtained."

As explained above, the self is not something that can be objectified or achieved. Achieving something means you have gained it, and it has the tendency to be lost; SELF is you yourself; it is YOU, and it is within YOU. Anything that has the nature of impermanence or tendency to be lost is not worth striving for. Ignorance impinges and draws a cloak over the pure Self, which is ecstasy. The idea or the notion behind the practices of knowing self and experiencing it is the mere effort to unveil the layers of worldly pleasures and evil that has had us in the fabricated identification of the SELF in the objectifying manner of the mind and the body. This false identification must go for the Self alone to remain; the pure, the true SELF.

"Therefore, realization is for everyone; realization makes no difference between the aspirants. This very doubt, whether you can realize, and the notion 'I-have-not-realized' are themselves the obstacles. Be free from these obstacles."

Awareness

What is this awareness, and how can one attain and promote it?

"You are aware. Awareness is another name for you. Since you are aware, there is no need to attain or cultivate it. All that you have to do is give up being aware of other

things that are of the not-self. If one gives up being aware of them, then pure awareness alone remains, and that is the Self. "

Attaining Self-Realization

Just like self, the realization is nothing to be achieved; it is already there within you. A human being is designed to have the element of realization within him or herself. All that is necessary to "realize" is to get rid of the negative thoughts, such as "I have not realized." The stillness, peace, and absoluteness is realization. There is no moment when you don't have the Self or the Awareness or Realization with you; everything is there under the layer of the though 'I have not realized.' As long as there is the thought of un-realization or doubts regarding your ability to realize, you will never be able to see through these thoughts.

We need to work upon removing this negativity or eliminating any such thoughts that we might have regarding the 'realization' to attain the wholeness of it. We need to make room for it in the chambers of our minds. How can we do that? By freeing up the space occupied by the negative thoughts and evil vibes. Your realization might certainly help you identify the blocks/hurdles of other people in their journey of self-realization and knowing the self. However, it is better for each person to experience it on their own. Just like nobody knows the actual worth of the gem better than the goldsmith, the same is with the realization and awareness of our own.

"When you identify yourself with the body, then only the forms and shapes are there. But when you transcend your body, the others disappear along with your body-consciousness."

Consciousness

Just as with the Self, people confuse consciousness with the other habits of natural human marvels. The sleep, dream, and waking conditions are mere wonders appearing on the Self, which is itself standing.

Just like Self, Consciousness is also a constant state of simple mindfulness. The question arises, "Am I nearer to myself in my sleep than in my waking state?"

Sri Ramana Maharishi answers this question in a beautiful manner: *"The Self is pure consciousness. No one can ever be away from the Self. The question is possible only if there is duality. But there is no duality in the state of pure consciousness. The same person sleeps, dreams, and wakes up. The waking state is considered to be full of beautiful and interesting things. The absence of such experience makes one say that the sleep state is dull."* He expounds on the example that signifies that there is a steadiness in the sleep and the waking state. That steadiness is the only state of pure existence. He explains the difference between the two conditions, saying that the incidents, specifically, the body, the world, and the objects, act in the waking state, but they vanish in sleep. People claim that they were not aware in their sleep, which is true. There is no consciousness of the body or of the worldly objects.

Sri Ramana Maharishi explains this recurrent question in the following words, *"You must exist in your sleep in order to say now 'I was not aware in my sleep.' Who says so now? It is the wakeful person. The sleeper cannot say so. That is to say, the individual who is now identifying the Self with the body says that such awareness did not exist in sleep. Because you identify yourself with the body, you see the world around you and say that the waking state is filled with beautiful and interesting things. The sleep state appears dull because you were not there as an individual, and therefore these things were not. But what is the fact? There is the continuity of being in all the three states, but no continuity of the individual and the objects."*

The process of self-development starts where self-actualization and self-realization begins.

"There is a life-force within your soul, seek that life. There is a gem in the mountain of your body, seek that mine. O traveler, if you are in search of that, don't look outside, look inside yourself, and seek that."

–Rumi

You are Co-creators with God

What establishes in life is where you place your devotion and awareness. If you keep your mindfulness and mind firm in the Light, what is to fear? The indolent mind is the devil's workshop. If you permit yourself to lose your attunement to God and the Masters, then it will float to the inferior self instead of your higher self, and this will root fear. It is only experienced by permitting yourself to be too much on autopilot and your mind too futile. Keep your mindfulness, mind, and activities always with God's attunement, God's thoughts, God's feelings, and God's activities, and no fear will ever emerge unless you allow it to. An enormous river of divine energy is flowing inside you right now. Those who have learned how to tap into this marvelous cradle of power appreciate a vastly different life than everyone else.

They see more deeply into other people, they are resistant to common difficulties and worries, and they can't help but attract genuine success to themselves wherever they go. By practicing meditation, you can discover how to touch this special river of vigor within yourself, and let it help you understand your highest ambitions.

So, to get started, I'd like to explain one crucial point. This energy isn't esoteric or mystical. You don't have to rely on "faith" to find it, and there are no mystical chants or imaginary visualizations required to have it "manifest" itself. The energy we're talking about is as real and tangible. It can be sensed and felt, as true as any other physical reality about you. In fact, you can even feel this energy as of right now by performing this simple exercise:

Settle down. Stop for a moment, whatever you are doing. Put aside everything you are holding. Sit back and relax. Take a deep breath, close your eyes, and exhale out any body tension. Start from the top, literally. Start by letting go of the tension in your head, then move it to the face, and step by step, part by part, move down to the neck and shoulders, then your arms and all the way down to your feet.

Once your body relaxes completely, a new form of stillness will appear. This stillness will replace the usual state of physical tension you possess most of the time. Just quietly notice this new energy and feel it throughout your body as it takes over gradually. This is fine energy pertaining to real-life experiences. Everything moves through its field, including the body, thoughts, and feelings.

"If you have previously thought that self-surrender meant giving up things and habits, you're really only seeing a small picture, a small portion of what you really have to do. On the higher level of self-surrender, it is not a giving up but rather, an accepting, accepting the Truth, accepting the Reality, accepting your Spiritual powers, your Spiritual Identity, your Spiritual Consciousness..."
-Herb Fitch 1980-81 Self Surrender Series

Chapter 5
The Spirit Knows What It Wants

Keshav temple, Somnathpur, Karnataka, South India

*"Sometimes, we are so overwhelmed by life that we don't
even know how to pray to God. Our words fail us because
of the depth of our pain or sorrow, but our prayer partner,
the Holy Spirit, can help us. The Apostle Paul says,
"Likewise the Spirit helps us in our weakness. For we do
not know what to pray for as we ought, but the Spirit
himself intercedes for us with groanings too deep for
words."*

-Romans 8:26

Your soul is leading you into certain circumstances and
relationships so you can remain connected with your soul's
true purpose. This instilled desire is more subconscious than

conscious. You are not vigorously thinking about it. So, it's very much like you are descending towards specific things that make sense to you, but you can't wrap your head around it. This has very little to do with the person you are or what you want – it is more connected to what you NEED.

If you seek to become mindful of yourself, you may entice other people in the form of relationships; this, however, may mirror back to you things about yourself. This reflection is significant for the growth of the soul. There is a force that follows you. It is a spiritual force that shadows the universal laws of nature. This force resides within you and guides your way. The best way to experience life at its optimum is to let yourself go with the flow of this force.

Your distinctive personality traits and the way you portray yourself as a person to others is the expression and origination of who you are as a spirit. Consciousness is not something attained; in fact, it can be anything. It is free of any limitations of expression or existence. And so are you, just like your consciousness. Your individual personality does not fix unless you restrict yourself. You are responsible for creating your own reality. It is you who control it – you can bend it, mend it, or change it for good. Whatever happens on the outer surface, is the reflection of what's undertaking within. The external world is an image of your inner world. All that you practice at the moment is an image of what you are in the present. If you change your being, you change your experience. In the mirror of the external world, we get to see the image of ourselves in appearance. That's why it is emphasized highly throughout, to turn within, to turn your life for good.

Energy is everywhere in every form. Everything around us releases vibrations at distinct frequencies. These vibrations exuberate energy in the form of packets, which then attract objects/incidents/events occurring at the same frequency. Energy is the core of that sits at the bottom of life and existence. We are designed to function in harmony with the pattern of a universal mind that serves the purpose of our existence. Energy is derived from our spiritual being in connection with the source energy. This universal mind seeks for balance; a balance that is symmetry and symmetry is perfection. The pattern of this universal mind is the flow of the spirit. Let loose your body, so may it follow the flow of the spirit. The spirit already knows what is best for you. It finds its purpose in the haystack. It navigates through your feelings and emotions, communicating through your senses in the form of motivation. Sometimes our lives get caught up in the midst of confusion. We become so indecisive of what we are doing and what we have to do. Even if we want to do certain things, our mind does not accompany the guts at times. This is due to a lack of motivation. When you follow the spirit, you do all the right things at the right time and save yourself from a lot of confusion. Your spirit is there to direct you. Listen to it, and you will never go wrong.

> *"At the center of your being*
> *you have the answer;*
> *you know who you are*
> *and you know what you want."*
> **-Lao Tzu**

Referring to the spirit means referring to a higher state of mind. Mind that is beyond the technicalities of rational/irrational thoughts. Your higher mind is in connection with the universal mind just as your subconscious is in connection with the superconscious. It knows everything about what's happening since it's linked with a divine connection. But how to know what spirit is telling you? Spirit dictates through the sixth sense and your gut. When we recite the words of positivity, it does nothing, since they are just mere syllables. What helps support them with a heavy overall impact is the strong feeling of positivity – the energy that comes with it.

The spirit liberates the desire that directs us to perform certain actions. We feel like doing what we are about to do. That desire is the inner prompt you need to follow to follow the spirit. Sometimes, this feeling or this urge is very subtle. So much so that it is almost overlooked by us humans. There is almost no force exercising itself upon you in either direction whatsoever. You are currently in a very balanced position where you can lean yourself in any direction.

That indicates that your soul is offering you the choice of free will with complete freedom of decision. When you look back after making the right decision, you would probably think that you almost might not have done what you did. It happened so freely as if by chance. The pace of the spirit is never too fast or hurried. Do not rush. Give yourself some time to reflect on the decisions that you are about to take or think for a while about what you are doing right now. Do not leave things to be done at the last moment. Take your time to complete tasks and never hurry. Hurry is the manifestation of fear and anxiety. It will instantly cut your connection with the universal mind. He who does not fear has a lot of time. Until you are not calm and your mind and body are not relaxed, you will gain no wisdom, knowledge, or power at all. Fear transforms all positive activities into negative ones, for instance, your strength into your weakness.

There is a difference in going at a fast pace and going in a hurry. When you hurry, you miss out on details. While when you are at a fast pace, you get to enjoy the details and experience every aspect of the details. Those who are wise about the spirit never seemed to hurry. They might be moving at a fast pace, but they experience every detail.

Live in the present. Live in the presence of mind and forget about the past. Do not worry about the future; just flow from one moment to the other patiently. Don't stress about what you wanted and what you did not get. If you did not get what you were seeking for, there sure is something better seeking you out. Maybe the actual original thing you were seeking in the first place was not the right time for you to have it. You may have what you wanted in the later part of your life.

You can create your own happiness and wipe away your own sadness. You can choose to either be the victim of despair or learn from the experiences and move on. You can choose to create your own reality. The power of death and life resides in the tongue. By tongue, we mean both physical and mental – the way your mind speaks. Your thoughts literally dictate your life and all the actions that you take.

Each person that is born desires to be born. He dies when that desire no longer lives.

Choose life so that you may live.

There's an unconscious agreement for death amongst groups of people who die in epidemics or natural disasters.

The power of epidemics affects those only who are in the same state. Those who do not choose to be involved, remain untouched even though being in the midst of it.

"A thousand may fall at your side and ten thousand at your right hand, but it shall not come near you. For he will deliver you from the snare of the fowler and from the deadly pestilence. He will cover you with his pinions, and under his wings, you will find refuge; his faithfulness is a shield and buckler. You will not fear the terror of the night, nor the arrow that flies by day, nor the pestilence that stalks in darkness, nor the destruction that wastes at noonday

-Psalm 91

In the case of immunization against any given disease, it is more of the belief and confidence and not the procedure that works. The immunization, while precisely effective, may only strengthen the belief that the body is futile on its own. Understanding Consciousness retains you from the fear of medical lack or unrelenting viruses.

The natural state of life itself is one of joy and accord with itself. It is a state in which action is effective, and the power to act is a natural right. No one really contends with each other but cooperates to form an environment in which all can creatively exist. The quality of life is important above all. All suffering is for the purpose of ending suffering and returning to harmony.

"Whatever you fear, keep it out of your mind and leave it in God's hands. Have faith in God. Much of the suffering is due only to worry. Why suffer before the disease actually shows up? Since most of our ailments come from fear, if you throw away all fear, you will be free instantly. Healing will be immediate. Every night, before you fall asleep, repeat this statement: "Divine Mother is with me; I am protected." Imagine yourself surrounded by the Spirit's cosmic energy, and think, "Every germ that attacks me will be electrocuted." Chant three times Om or the word "God"; this will act like a shield and you will feel the wonderful

divine protection. Let go of fear and negativity, it's the only way to be healthy. If you commune with God, truth will flow to you and you will know that you are actually the imperishable soul."
-Paramahansa Yogananda

Chapter 6
The Science of Kriya Yoga

***An Insight to Interrelationship between
Science and Spirituality***

*"The Western day is indeed nearing when the inner science
of self-control will be found as necessary as the outer
conquest of nature. This new Atomic Age will see men's
minds sobered and broadened by the now scientifically
indisputable truth that matter is, in reality, a concentrate of
energy."*
-Paramahansa Yogananda

Why do we always swing between landing onto either one
of the both; science or spirituality? The closest and most
essential definition of science is the explanation of how

things are. Universal Laws function throughout the universe. The difference is to be conscious of those laws to be able to understand how things work. Science and faith do not contradict each other. In fact, they both support each other through facts and patterns.

The best way to understand faith, in fact, is to approach it through science. This way, we will not be able to just understand it, but also apprehend what goes behind. All spiritual and paranormal phenomena can be scientifically explained. Science discovers the nonphysical dynamics and the true nature of the universe that evolves to a higher order.

There are common principles that underpin different perspectives and methods of faith. When we discover these principles, we discover the underlying truth. No religion is higher than that truth. The truth is the only reality that is omnipresent. God is truth, and God is all that is. And since the ultimate truth is that all is one, it is harmonizing and connecting.

When it comes to mental and physical health, everyone wants to stay ahead of their time. Being in the limelight for a very long time now, the link or relationship between spirituality and medical health care has increasingly gone under the microscope. Many known researchers have carried out experiments and examined behavioral changes in the light of spiritual guidance and meditation practices. So much so that now it is considered as conventional wisdom that spirituality is linked with better mental, physical, and emotional health.

Concluding the several results obtained from various researches and studies, there were a few points that were common in every finding. These points were the experiences recorded from the patients (subjects) who went under the observation and experiment for the study based on spiritual guidance and meditation practice. Undeniably, the results were noticeable as they recorded their feelings in the following words:

- Patients say they have gained better self-control.
- Patients' self-esteem and self-confidence received a boost, and they became more comfortable in their skin.
- Patients concluded spiritual guidance and proper meditation led to their faster recovery (from past grieves, losses, and weaknesses).

- The subjects of the study recorded that they have noted a significant change in their behavior, specifically with their spouse. Somehow, from the study, they have grown to become better at relationships, making stronger and healthier bonds with their partners as well as with their God and nature itself.

- In addition to that, patients stated that they have come out of the study phase as a better person overall, inside out. They felt rejuvenated, contented, and had this utter realization of the peace of mind – peace of mind which they had been craving for so long.

- Last but not least, patients claimed that their decision-making ability had improved multiple folds. They are now not just better at making decisions (without getting any second thoughts or anxiety), but their analytical skills have sharpened as well.

In the western world, the practice of doing yoga has come to symbolize serenity, calmness, peace, and the state of well-being. It had been practiced in the east for centuries;

however, the recent trend observed in the west shows more and more people are becoming aware of this technique to improve health, internal and external, as well as the overall quality of life. This mind-body practice is frequently preached and practiced due to its long list of incredible health benefits as well as self-growth. The number one reason people seek the practice of yoga and meditation is that they are known for reducing stress and anxiety and putting the mind and soul at peace. The benefits don't end there. With regular practice, people experience a boost in their well-being other than all the mental and physical health benefits.

At Self Realization Fellowship (SRF) Los Angeles, California

Kriya yoga taught by Swami Parmahansa Yogananda is a branch of Yoga that stems out from the hundreds of years old eastern practice and has now gained a lot of popularity in the west. Kriya yoga serves as a tool to quicken human evolution. Ancient yogis discovered that the secret to cosmic consciousness lies within mastering your breathing. Kriya yoga is said to be the greatly advanced Raja Yoga technique of pranayama. The practice spreads its magic around the domain of the spine and the brain. It revitalizes your inner systems and reinforces subtle currents of life energy, known as Prana, in the spine and the brain.

According to western medicine, the major and most numbers of human disease are either due to or somehow linked to the brain or the spinal cord. Rishis (the ancient Indian seers) perceived the brain and the spine as the tree of life, which is very well and beautifully explained. Energies that evoke a sense of life and rejuvenates everything as it passes, flows through the subtle cerebrospinal centers of life and consciousness (chakras), refreshing every tissue, every organ, and every tissue of the body. The yogis discovered that by the special technique of kriya yoga, revolving/flowing life current continuously up and down the spine, one's spiritual awareness and evolution can be greatly accelerated.

In addition to that, if practiced correctly, with full concentration and focus, kriya yoga slows down the systems of your body, putting it to comfort. The normal activities of lungs, nerves, and heart systems are slowed down naturally. This produces deep inner stillness of mind and body, diverting the attention completely from the chaos inside one's self and also in the surroundings. This removes a person's attention from the usual turbulence, emotions, thoughts, and sensory perceptions.

At that moment – in clarity of that inner stillness – one reaches a point where he or she experiences a deepening inner peace and the attunement with God and one's soul. Moreover, anybody can practice kriya yoga by their own self or with the teaching of a guru (this is more preferable for the beginners). However, since everything goes systematically, the technique of kriya yoga is taught to the students of self-realization fellowship lessons who have applied to receive the magic or kriya yoga after the preliminary period of studying and practicing the first three techniques taught by Yogananda.

Those three techniques are

- Energization Exercises
- Hong-Sau Technique of Concentration
- Aum Technique of Meditation

History of Kriya Yoga

Kriya yoga science's meditation techniques, which form the foundation of the Kriya Yoga path, date back to ancient times – as ancient as human civilization. As old as they are, these practices are still perfectly suited to the contemporary world. The modern world is in dire need of guidance, encouragement, support, love, and joy of the divine that can be attained through daily meditation. The science of Kriya Yoga is universal – one fit for all. "Saadhna" is the name given to the spiritual discipline of meditation practices and teachings regarding 'how to live' by Paramahansaji. These are stated and taught in the Self-Realization Fellowship Lessons. Any true seeker that holds the love for the spiritual power in his/her heart and is a firm believer of God can have a direct experience of God after fulfillment.

Benefits of Kriya Yoga

Each and every single benefit obtained by the yoga practice is interrelated to some other discipline or conduct of life. This number multiplies if we consider all the benefits of yoga and meditation. Similarly, there are multiple advantages of Kriya yoga. There's a chemical reaction that goes into our mind and body when we perform certain tasks with full concentration and goal. Through regular practice of the Kriya yoga path of meditation, subtle packets of transformation occur in the human body, mind, and his or her inmost consciousness.

Moreover, some of these consequential benefits are experienced right away since day first of the very first session. However, some other in-depth benefits take time to unfold completely; it's like you are stepping onto each successive level one after another, unlocking the new ones by the time as you proceed further. They apparently take more time to become apparent and evolve progressively. Some of the additional benefits of Kriya Yoga are mentioned below:

- Inner Peace – no matter how much I emphasize this point, it won't be enough to justify the impact it has on one's inner state of mind. This is the ripest fruit of the Kriya Yoga tree that is obtained from meditation.

- Greater clarity of mind and a better understanding of situations and guidance from within.

- It enhances your analytical skills.

- Develops the instincts to address the problems that arise in everyday life. It improves your understanding and thinking capability to critically judge and identify the problem to address for the possible solutions.

- Sparks intuitive knowledge and brings objectivity in the course of conduct.

- It clears the way and banishes any barriers blocking the pores of concentration. It increases efficiency and generates a willingness to work with greater efforts.

- It adds the missing spark to the relationships by restoring the faith and the joy in family life; it awakens the capacity to give and receive unconditional love.

- Kriya yoga harmonizes the life forces in the body, promoting healthy vitality and terminating any left behind traces of harmful stress.

- Most importantly, it attunes one's consciousness with the divine/God and His powers. This results in an unshakable belief in nature and the sense of happiness and security amidst any circumstances in life.

However, to obtain these overwhelmingly beneficial results, one must prepare himself or herself mentally for what he or she is stepping into. These results require sincere outputs and regular processes of meditation practices by mobilizing the will to continue to strive towards the ultimate goal in life.

Swami Paramahansa Yogananda

"Bliss—which is God, man's ultimate goal—is felt in an intense degree in the practice of Kriya Yoga. The practice of Kriya is far more purely blissful than the greatest enjoyment that any of our five senses or the mind can ever afford us. I do not wish to give anyone any other proof of this truth than is afforded by his own experience. The more one practices Kriya with patience and regularity, the more one feels intensely and durably fixed in Bliss, or God.
-Swami Paramahansa Yogananda

As a reference from **Bhagavad Gita,** Hindus' biggest prophet Krishna, referred to Kriya Yoga as:

"Offering inhaling breath into the outgoing breath, and offering the outgoing breath into the inhaling breath, the yogi neutralizes both these breaths; he thus releases the life force from the heart and brings it under his control."

The interpretation is: "The yogi arrests decay in the body by an addition of life force, and arrests the mutations of growth in the body by apan (eliminating current). Thus neutralizing decay and growth, by quieting the heart, the yogi learns life control." We have six spinal centers known as medullary, dorsal, sacral, lumbar, cervical, and coccygeal plexuses.

What kriya yoga does is, it mentally directs the life energy to revolve in all possible motions (upward, downwards, inwards, outwards, etc.) around these centers. Just a one or half-minute of this revolution of energy around the sensitive nodes of the spinal cord affects subtle evolution in a man's progress; this half-minute of Kriya is an equivalent of one-year natural spiritual unfoldment.

Kriya enables the outgoing life force to be constrained to reunite with other, subtler spinal energies. The yogi's brain cells and the whole body, thus, are kind of rejuvenated or electrified with the spiritual elixir. Kriya unties the breath cord that holds the soul to the body – chained together, bounding each other. It frees the soul and body from the shackles of limited breathing that, in turn, serves to enlarge the consciousness to infinity and prolonged life. These yoga methods serve as a key that enables one to overcome the constant battle between the matter-bound senses and the mind. It frees the one practicing and renders him to re-inherit the eternal kingdom. He knows its true nature, which is neither bounded by breath limitation nor by physical encasement.

Chapter 7
Sant-Mat and Meditation Practice

Lightning flashed in my eye, O friend,
And brightly did shine the light of the moon.
I got a glimpse of the Invisible within,
And thirst and longing for the Lord were aroused.
My ears received the boon of Unstruck Music, And
Knowledge came like the explosion of light, O Friend.
Dark clouds began to scatter and the sight
Of the Divine Mansion was revealed unto me.
Beyond the sun, the moon and the tunnel,
Tulsi beheld the abode of the Lord Almighty.
-Glimpse of the Invisible -- Mystic Verses of Sant Tulsi
Sahib

The main subject of the topic that we are discussing here

is the meditation practices by Sant Mat, **the light and sound**

meditation (Also taught in Kriya Yoga). The meditation

practice of inner spiritual light and sound is now being recognized and taught globally and is not just popular in the United States. Tens of thousands of people from different walks of life are being taught the meditation practice of Sant Mat.

What is Sant Mat?

Sant Mat, the living school of spirituality, is also referred to as the way of Poet-Mystics, the path of saints, and the path of Masters. This age-old spiritual way of lifestyle includes developing trust, love, and respect for all. The Sant Mat lifestyle is in harmony with higher value, and the main notion that it encompasses is discovering our full potential as true human beings. These are the values that nurture our soul through meditation – regular contact with the inner light and sound.

To build a channel to access this contact through a medium, you require adequate and authentic guidance. This guidance is better if achieved through the instructor or any spiritual teacher. It is its positive, impactful results that millions of people from diversified religions, cast, nations, and cultures are learning and adapting to more and more.

Says Tulsi, Hear me O Taqi, the inner secret is unlike anything you have known before. Keep it safe in your heart, for it focuses you on the Most High [God].

Meditation Practice – What Goes Behind?

I felt like before we delve into an in-depth, detailed study of Sant Mat meditation practice and the principles of the study, I should tell my readers its background. This will help you develop a better understanding. The devotee must be able to control his or her mind and then meditate the Word, also known as Surat Dharana. This means to control the mind with Internal Mystical Sound Current.

"Man shall not live by bread alone, but by every word that comes from the mouth of God."
-Matthew 4:4

This is the basic step for beginners. It will enable them to cut away the surrounding distractions and have better control of their mind when the mind is focused on the word (inner sound). And when your mind does not wander off of the word, you can say it is under control now. Once the mind is under control, the devotee can meditate. In such a meditation, the meditator realizes their 'oneness' with the meditation object. Meditation is similar to pouring a viscous liquid out of a bottle (consider honey, for example). Whenever you pour a viscous liquid out, it never breaks and keeps falling into a consistent, continuous motion, until every drop has come out of it. The next step now for the devotee is to attain self-realization. The next loop of the chain is to learn the Samadhi. There are different sorts of samadhis that project for different distinctive goals.

Similarly, in Nirvikalpa Samadhi (Highest State of Samadhi), God, Soul, and the Meditator become One. Once these states are attained, a person feels an instant sense of liberation. The meditator realizes oneness with God during his or her lifetime. His thoughts, his actions, his words, and thinking, everything becomes harmonious, and he experiences utter joy.

Then how does the soul merge into God?

Once a devotee inquires a Sat-Guru (A true teacher/a person who is considered to have achieved enlightenment, and who can help others to achieve the same) regarding how the Surat (attention of soul) and Shabd (the sound current) come to a person? He asked, how can the Surat be pure and love the shabda? He added more to his question and asked about how all the differences get abolished when the soul merges into the universal Word. To this question, the Satguru replied in a very understanding manner. He said:

"When all the thought waves merge into the Divine *Sound, they become Sound. There are no more thoughts. Only Word remains. The Surat and Shabda cannot then be differentiated. When the Surat unites with Shabda, it is just as when water mixes with the milk and become one. Surat gives up its own identity and merges into the Word. Although Surat and Shabda appear different, they are not really separate. Once the union has occurred, and the thought waves are silenced, bliss is experienced. When the waters of two rivers such as the Ganges and the Yamuna unite at Prayag, one cannot differentiate the waters; just so, when Surat and Shabda unite, they are indistinguishable. However, for this to occur, one has to meditate before that Oneness can be realized. The Yamuna merges into the Ganges and loses itself, and only the Ganges remains. In the same way, when Surat merges into Shabda, then only Shabda remains. No one can then identify any separation or differences. When one attains unity with Shabda, his surati becomes pure. All the passions of lust, anger, attachment, greed, and ego are removed. He becomes a true devotee."*
-Shri Prakash Mani, From the "Prakash Mani Gita," on Surat Shabd Yoga Sadhana (Inner Light and Sound Meditation Practice)

From Inner Light to Sound

The path leading to God lies within you; God is not found in manmade buildings. Rather, to find Him, you need to enter the third eye chakra. He is found inside your heart. This is because your inner self is the holy place where there is God.

You need to TURN YOUR ATTENTION WITHIN!

Listen closely to the vibrations and frequencies that run inside you and around you. Pay close attention to the divine sounds. The reverberating sound you hear is coming to take you back. But wait, you need not hear this through your physical ears. Someone who thinks he can listen to these sounds through his ear is bewildered. As you cannot see the consciousness with your physical eyes, you cannot listen to these harmonics through your ears. When you focus your gaze with the help of a chakra, your consciousness will be diverted inwards. What does this mean? This means that your physical ears will automatically be closed to the worldly noises and pollution, and your inner ears will be open. This way, you will be able to cancel all the surrounding voices that may cause an interruption in your meditation. Through this power, you can listen to the celestial sounds with your inner ears. The original sounds of the creation come from the abode of God, and it will take you to Him.

Dr. Julian Philip Matthew Johnson, an American surgeon, and author of several books on Eastern spirituality, spent much of the 1930s in India studying Sant Mat and Surat Shabd Yoga.

In his book 'The Path of the Masters' Dr. Julian Johnson talked of this sound current this way:

"The audible life stream is the cardinal, central fact in the science of the masters... it is the supreme fact and factor of the entire universe. It is the very essence and life of all things. It is perhaps less known than any other important fact of nature, yet it is the one determining factor of all nature. That is indeed a pity." This audible life stream is even talked about in the Gospel of John.

"In the beginning was the Word, and the Word was with God, and the Word was God. The same was in the beginning with God. All things were made by him and without him was not anything made that was made."
(John 1:1-3)

Sant Kabir said: *'Close your eyes, ears, and mouth, and listen to the anahad* (inner Unstruck Divine Sound).'

Initially, we receive the teaching by using our hearing sense, but once we fully believe in it, it becomes our intuitive hearing. As our desire to attain Samadhi and wisdom heightens in the mind, we can certainly avail it by the intuitive hearing.

Sants have depicted about the closing of the three gates of the body to delve with the inner sound. The three gates being eyes, ears, and mouth. Close these in unison, and only then can you hear your inner sound. Close the three gates and indulge in the divine sound.

Sant Nanak Sahab says: *"Close the three gates and listen to the reverberation of the Divine Sound."*

Sant Maharshi Mehi and also Sufi Sants have used similar vocabulary to describe the process of closing three openings for hearing the inner Sound.

"Someone asked, 'If the **Sound** is not heard with the physical ears, then with what kind of ear is this subtle Sound heard?' When the mind becomes concentrated, then the physical sense of hearing becomes quiet, and one does not hear. This occurs because the attention withdraws from the senses, and one is unable to hear the physical sound.

Sant Tulsi Sahab says: *"A practitioner who is able to focus in the Sushumna or the tenth gate for some time will experience the opening of the inner subtle hearing faculty. That inner sense of hearing is also known as the consciousness Current."*

Guru Maharshi Mehi said: *"A practitioner hears the sweet Sound of the flute through the stream of inner consciousness.' When the outer ear ceases to hear, and the mind is fully concentrated within, then the inner hearing opens up, and the practitioner can hear the Divine Sound within (through the inner ear)...*

"By focusing on the third eye he must attempt to recognize the Central Sound, as instructed by the guru. As soon as the practitioner recognizes the Sound emanating from the center of the light realm, this Sound, like a magnet, will attract the consciousness and will draw it to the center of a higher realm. Once a practitioner grasps the Central Sound, he will continue to ascend upward until the soul reaches the ultimate goal of realization of the Divine.

Maharshi Mehi says: *"It might be possible to separate the magnet from the iron but the consciousness Current which is attracted to the Divine Sound cannot be separated in spite of any outward distractions and dangers."*

Sant Daria Sahab elaborates: *"My mind is always drawn to the Divine Sound (Shabd) and it has forsaken all worldly distractions. Day and night, it is focused on the target and listens to the resounding of the Divine Sounds (Shabd) within."*

— Swami Vyasanand Ji Maharaj, The Inward Journey of the Soul (Chal Hansa Nij Desh)

According to Surangama Sutra, Sacred Text of Mystical Buddhism:

"At first we receive this teaching through our sense of hearing, but when we are fully able to realize it, it becomes ours through a Transcendental and Intuitive Hearing. This makes the awakening and perfecting of a transcendental faculty of hearing of very great importance to every novice. As the wish to attain Samadhi deepens in the mind of any disciple, he can most surely attain it by means of his Transcendental Organ of Hearing. How sweetly mysterious is the Transcendental Sound of Avalokiteshvara! It is the pure Brahman Sound. It is the subdued murmur of the seatide setting inward. Its mysterious Sound brings liberation and peace to all sentient beings who, in their distress, are calling for aid; it brings a sense of permanency to those who are truly seeking the attainment of Nirvana's Peace."

"The Nadabindu Upanishad" sings the praise of [inner] Sound Yoga and offers this image:

'When a mad (in a rut) elephant goes to a banana orchard and destroys and eats the orchard, and the elephant keeper comes and pierces the elephant with a prong, the elephant is brought under control. In the same manner, our mind is like the mad elephant that is wandering in the garden of sense objects and is disciplined by the practice of [inner] Sound Yoga.'

An Opening to the Realms of Inner Light!

"This calls for a motionless, still gazing ahead right in front of the center of the two eyes in the inner dark void that is seen upon closing our eyes gently. The art of gazing in the inner dark vastness that the currents of consciousness

present in the two eyes, meet at a point, so the gaze gets fixed in a Point, has to be learned from an accomplished Guru, and practiced regularly with utmost faith and sincerity. It must be noted here that Sants warn strictly against any kind of imagining of the presence of a Point within.

Whenever the two currents meet, a bright Point is automatically seen – it does not have to be imagined or visualized. Whenever this happens, breathing adjusts automatically. Awareness of own body and surroundings is lost even as the meditator is fully alert and conscious internally. Ascension or transcendence is a direct corollary of concentration. As a result, thus, of awareness shrinking completely into an absolute Point, the 'jiva' or 'surat' (non-liberated individual soul that is combined with the mind, etc...) pierces through or transcends the gross sphere, and ascends into the astral sphere where countless varieties of Sounds called Anahad ('ana' meaning 'no,' and 'had' meaning limit or boundary) Nada (Sounds) are heard. Brilliant lights, innumerable worlds, stars, moon, sun, advanced souls, etc.... etc.... are seen by the practitioner, who has become completely oblivious of or has left behind the gross universe (that his physical body exists in) behind.

The soul keeps flying in the inner sky like a bird, sighting all the magnificent scenes. Hence Bindu Dhyan or the Yoga of Light is also known as the 'vihangam marg' (vihangam means 'bird,' and marg means 'path'). The perceiver becomes indescribably enthralled, ecstatic by the mesmerizing sights. But he has to move on, resisting these temptations, and rise still further to accomplish his ultimate goal, which is Self-Realization or God-Realization."

-From the Preamble of, Yoga of Inner Light and Sound, by Swami Achyutanand, translated by Pravesh K. Singh

Meditation Practices (Sadhana) According to Sant Mat Mysticism

There are several meditation practices in Sant Mat. All of which comprise of several techniques, specific details of which are taught to the students. These teachings and techniques are usually taught at the initial level of the meditation practices to the beginners.

First things first, to be habitual of any practice, you need to develop a daily routine. It is imperative for meditation to be effective if it is given sufficient time. And, more importantly, to make sure that you give the same time slot to it each day without compromising its schedule with any otherworldly distractions.

- Maintain a proper posture with your back straight so that your whole attention span is focused at the third eye and remains alert and awake. As discussed earlier, sitting in a comfortable position holds immense importance in the procedure of meditation. Your body needs to be at peace so that your journey towards peace of mind and soul is easy.

- Manas Japa (Simran) – a repeated mantra recited mentally.

- Manas Dhyan – practicing to visually perceive God, and Seeing Him as one's teacher.

- Practice Drishti Yoga – the yoga of inner light. This is the technique of focusing upon an infinitesimal point. The point will gradually blossom into inner light or visions of light. One gaze into the middle of the darkness or the Light one sees while in meditation. To develop a better understanding, think of this infinitesimal point as being a laser beam that is pointing in a singular dimension, keeping one focused. One passes from scene to scene, with different displays appearing before him, looking towards the center.

- Nadanusandhana – the yoga of inner sound. This is also known as the practice of inner spiritual hearing.

- Kaivalya: reaching this state means to share the wholeness with the Supreme. Simply put, it is the pure conscious realm.

"The Lord is in me, the Lord is in you, as life is in every seed, put false pride away, and seek the Lord within..."
-Sant Kabir

Teachings of Sant Mat – The Path of Masters

By now, you must have got a great idea about what Sant Mat is. How does it operate? And what are the teachings of it?

There are seven core notions that sit at the core of Sant Mat teachings, which are mentioned below:

- There is God.
- God is Love.
- Everything in this world, and all the scriptures that we have, provide us teachings about the same

manifestation of God for He is the inner light and the mystical sound.

- Our only and true identity is the identity of Soul, the identity of self. The soul is the part of God, and thus it is as pure as God; pure love.

- We have an opportunity to experience God within this human existence.

- We can explore our inner space and rise above body-consciousness. It all happens as we begin with the love of God during meditation and discover the "Kingdoms of havens that are within us. We travel back from the Realm of Darkness to the realm of light, from the light to divine sound, and from the realm of sound to the soundless state" - (Sant Sevi Ji Maharaj). This drop merges back into the ocean of love.

- As we go further and further, unfolding the mysteries of the spirit with the aid of a Living Teacher (Sant Satguru), the purpose of our life is fulfilled. Our life becomes more and more complete, filling in the gaps of what's been missing from it for so long as we begin to reunite with God.

"It was for the sake of the God-conscious beings that our True Lord created this earth, and began this play of death and birth."

-Adi Granth

Ultimate Reality is beyond any beginning or end, infinite, beyond birth, beyond the senses, all-pervading yet even beyond pervasiveness. It must, therefore, be understood as the Supreme Being. This Essential Element is known in Sant mat as the Lord of All and is the foundation of all things. This Being is beyond both the inanimate and animate aspects of nature. It is without qualities and beyond qualities. Its nature is infinite, imperishable, all-powerful. It is beyond time and space, beyond sound and beyond form (Nirguna). It is the One without a second.

The Supreme Being is beyond the scope of the mind, the intellect and the senses. This entire universe is powered by the energy of this Being. This Being is not human. It is not manifested in physical form. It has existence beyond the illusion of maya [illusion], and there is nothing that exists outside of it. It is the Being which is eternal and is in existence from the beginning. Sant mat considers this Being

to be the Divine Reality, and this [knowing or merging with]
this Being is the goal of all spirituality.

-*Swami Sant Sevi Ji Maharaj*

Kabir says: "For millions of years you have slept. This
morning, will you not wake?"

Chapter 8
Search of God

Don't look for the God in the sky; Search for your Self, and you'll find him in your heart!

"If the Creator stood before a million men with the light of a million lamps, only a few would truly see him because the truth is already alive in their hearts. Those with truth in them can only see the truth. He who does not have Truth in his heart will always be blind to it."

-Suzy Kassem

Are we all searching for God? If not, then we are searching for a life leading to true fulfillment. We desire love, and to be loved, we want to belong and be associated.

Have you ever wondered what life is actually about and what is its purpose? As soon as you type, "Where is God?" in the search engine, millions of results will pop up, only to increase your insecurity and anxiousness that millions before you have had the same questions. Why does it seem so hard to find God? Where do we lack? What is it that we are doing wrong that is not bringing us the desired results?

"See what love the Father has given us, that we should be called children of God, and that is what we are."
-1 John 3:1

God is our Creator. Be assured that you are never alone in any situation. Knowing that you are a loving child of God brings you a sense of security, familiarity, freedom, and strength. Sharing a bond with God brings you a source of endless love and companionship.

"Our Father who art in HEAVEN, Hallowed be thy NAME. Thy kingdom come. Thy WILL be done on earth, as it is in heaven. Give us this day our daily BREAD. And forgive us our DEBTS, as we forgive our debtors. And lead us not into TEMPTATION, but deliver us from EVIL: For thine is the KINGDOM, and the POWER, and the GLORY, forever. Amen."
- Matthew 6:9-13

Asking about the whereabouts of God is a very common question. It is a great question that raises a sense of knowing. It is one of those questions many people seek answers for different reasons. The answer might not be the same for everyone, but it sure will be right. The search for God is often triggered if the person is seeking forgiveness, validation for life, is in deep sorrow, is enjoying a great joy of life, or wants to know the meaning or the purpose of life. Sometimes it springs from validation. At other times, we look for God if we are looking for someone to blame or when we are in doubt. It may begin from intellectual curiosity, trying to apprehend and capture big questions like the purpose of life.

Where is God, and how can we talk to him? Where is God when there is so much pain and suffering in the world? All these uncertainties try to cast doubts in our perceptions and on the existence of God. As I have said before, in this materialistic world, we are blinded by the phenomenon of the growth of worldly pleasures, our physical features, and wealth and possession, so much so that we lose our true purpose of existence. As concerned as we are about growth, we should equally be conscious of our spiritual learning.

Spiritual learning and progress encapsulate both an enhanced understanding of the relation between God and creation and a definite improvement in our capacities for better lives. The system has placed a lot of reinforcement in escaping physical existence, to the extent that spiritual things appear as intangible or out of the reach of the mind and body, disconnected from normal life.

> *"To follow God, one must be a little "out of their mind" (and "into their Spirit").*
>
> ***-Donald L. Hicks***

The quote implies that before you embark on finding God, you need to be free of the shackles of mind that are constricting your belief system. You should be comfortable experiencing new experiences. You should embrace the search of God with an open mind and an accepting heart. Could our minds experience deep intimacy? The reality we breathe in is the illusion that our eyes seek. But what our eyes fail to see is the reality within reality – a reality that is crawling beneath the thin air we breathe, a reality that is disguised by the thick mist of quantized rational facts and figures, a reality in hindsight.

Our minds perceive what we believe. We see what we are shown, but what about the unseen that is hidden? What about the reality that is yet to be experienced by our minds? Every human being on this earth's surface was born to serve a purpose. You were not just born to survive, live an average life, seek what is told, and then leave this body. My life experience nurtured my search to understand this in a new light. It evoked a sense of awakening, which enabled me to think parallel to experience. Now, I not only think about my thoughts but can experience the preciousness of life, which was impossible for me to interpret before with my underdeveloped mental perception.

We are so blinded by rationality that we fail to seek what lies beyond us. The "normal" is the problem. What do you mean by having something in a normal state? Does it imply being in a state that is coherent to the preconceived worldly notions? Or is it the term given to thinking limitation – limitations that are shackled to the thinking capability? What would it be like to have a state of mind that sustains and maintains a state of oneness with all life? Imagine what would be possible if you had exercises that constantly repaired the fragmented aspects of the mind that have kept your thinking so busy and preoccupied with worries and confusion? This has impaired your ability to think beyond the reality, to explore the events that enfold within; your thinking is streamed in a single dimension only.

Without the mind functioning properly, you do not realize you are rarely present to life much less in touch with the unity of all life. You are dwelling in this realm of confusion. Why don't we develop our minds to serve as a platform, not just to think about numbers and figures, but also to reflect upon the aspects of nature and creation and the beauty, wonder, and delight in everything?

The sense of awareness and the sense of inner realization is what can bring out the external results. Only from within can we bring the balance, a stable estimate of what is worth it. The sense of appreciation of this inner realization depends majorly on the understanding of the inner SELF, the realization of Your Self to God, and the others.

St. Peter's Basilica, Vatican City, Rome

Prayer and Meditation
Prayer

How do you define prayer? Is prayer just performing repetitive acts prescribed by ancestors, or does prayer have any significance of its own? Some people do not give in very much to the thought of either prayer or meditation. They are satisfied with a very little amount of information that their minds possess and like to go with the flow without stressing any coordinates, hoping that somehow, somewhere the conditions will work out the best for them. On the contrary, some enthusiasts are in constant search of guidance, hope, and answers. They seek information and entail realities that enfold within a subject. In seeking in-depth knowledge, they attain a better understanding of their present lot and justification for the life course that is pursued. You can refer to prayer as a call to God.

Unlike the daily murmurings of the vast majority of mankind in all lands who by their vain repetitions hope to gain the ear of God, prayer is the ecstasy of a spiritual wedding taking place in the deep, silent stillness of consciousness." – Neville

Prayer sends a signal to God/Divine intelligence, conveying what you ask for. Prayer is a communication between the creator and the creation. It enables a follower, to burn all the gaps, and connect directly to God Himself. In other words, it is the concentrated effort to be attuned to the Creator's consciousness.

So how can we attune ourselves? Through prayers, we can channel our minds to the spiritual strengths and forces existing in this world around us. It could also be the unified experience, shared mutually by many individuals, coming together with a unified thinking mind. Prayer, for some, is just the outer experience to be seen and praised by the others. However, to others, it is about the cleansing of the inner body, mind, and heart. Through prayer, one can enter the zone of eternal bliss, exhaling out the ego so that the inner being can fill with spiritual healing. Christ defines this different pattern of examples in the following words:

"Two men went up into the temple to pray, the one a Pharisee, and the other a publican. The Pharisee stood and prayed thus with himself, God, I thank thee, that I am not as other men are, extortions, unjust, adulterers, or even as this publican. I fast twice in the week. I give tithes of all that I possess. And the publican, standing afar off, would

not lift so much as his eyes unto heaven, but smote upon his breast, saying, God be merciful to me a sinner. I tell you, [said Jesus] this man went down to his house justified rather than the other."

-Luke 18:10-14

Meditation

What is meditation? It is an open-ended question with no definitive answers restricting to just one-dimensional possibility. However, it does have some common principles that you will find among all the answers. Meditation develops the instincts to address the problems that arise in everyday life. It improves your understanding and your thinking capability to critically judge and identify problems and find possible solutions.

Meditation sparks intuitive knowledge and brings objectivity in the course of conduct. It clears the way and banishes any barriers blocking concentration. It increases efficiency and generates a willingness to work with greater efforts. It adds the missing spark to relationships by restoring faith and joy in family life; it awakens the capacity to give and receive unconditional love. As long as you are new to meditation and spiritual art, certain formalized meditations can do good for the initial learning process of your mind.

However, if you are a seeker of reality, there is only one meditation, the rigorous refusal to harbor thoughts. You need to be free of thoughts clogging up your brain's path from thinking in other dimensions. To be free from thoughts or to cut away extra thoughts burdening your mind is itself a form of meditation.

"You begin by letting thoughts flow and watching them. The very observation slows down
The mind until it stops altogether. Once the mind is quiet, keep it quiet. Don't get bored with
peace, be in it; go deeper into it.
                                        -Sri Nisargadatta Maharishi

Meditation is the cleansing of mind and our thinking ability. Worldly distractions that constrict our minds, hindering spiritual forces from affecting us, are all filtered out through meditation practice.

We begin to experience new zones of reality as soon as meditation rewards us in return. We begin to sense new feelings of power, strength, and emotional, mental, and physical stability.

"He went in the strength of that meat received for many days." (281-13)

Many people fall into believing meditation is the same as daydreaming or musing. However, meditation is all about attuning our whole being with the spiritual source. It brings us to the straight path from where we have gone astray. Meditation attunes our disruptive patterns of living a life and brings together all the scattered pieces, forming a streamline of strengthened mind peace and eternal bliss.

Meditation enables our mental and physical bodies to be in sync with the spiritual source. It induces the realization of expression; a relationship shared by the man with their maker. This is what true meditation is. Meditation is also prayer, but sort of like a prayer from within. It is the prayer from the soul, the prayer from the inner self. It is not only for the benefit of the physical body but is also for the soul and the spirit.

Whenever we pray, we express to God/Higher Power that we are anxious for His blessings, His guidance, and His help for the manifestation of the promises in our lives. The next phase of prayer is obtaining the attitude of wait and patience, where you wait for what you asked for to happen. It is the phase where one waits for his or her call to be answered by the Heavenly God. It is the attitude of waiting in silence, to be able to hear the small voice within in the form of a response to one's query and to know that everything is going to be alright. Thus, prayer is the basis of meditation.

Only when we are still, we can know God, and when we know Him, we are willing to say and mean, "Thy will be done."

Prayer is the preliminary stage or a prerequisite to meditation. Prayer is the stairway to the platform of meditation, where one develops a sense of strengthened bond with the master of his creation.

Preparation for Meditation

We have briefly discussed how to prepare for meditation previously. Since the topic is so widespread and lays the basic foundation for the concept of this whole book, I felt there was a need for us to discuss it in-depth, covering the aspects of preparation of mind, body, and soul. Through meditation, we can trace our lives back, connecting to our inner source to get to know the true essence of being alive.

Meditation develops the instincts to address the problems that arise in everyday life.

It improves your understanding and thinking – the capability to judge and identify the problem to find solutions. It sparks intuitive knowledge and brings objectivity in conduct. Meditation is an art. It takes away your soul from one dimension to another, putting it at rest. Meditation is where the soul finds its peace, and you find your SELF. Meditation takes away your senses for a while into another world, away from all this world's noises and interruptions. If done right, the delicate meditation practice can open a portal for wonders to seep into your life.

Let's look at some notions that need to be addressed when preparing for meditation. We all depict a miniature model of the universe, processing mental, spiritual, and physical chambers within us. These chambers or these bodies are so closely knit together that one affects the other two. Manifesting in this world surrounded by materialism, the physical human body is a composite unit of creative force. And it is not just the human body; in fact, everything in this universe possesses the same attributes of a miniature universe within them – a replica. A famous saying declares that "your body is like a temple," and thus, you must act accordingly. You would never want to enter a temple if you are not clean, nor would you like its inner space to be polluted by any means. It is not only our duty to know ourselves but to explore and to discover the depths of our consciousness, mindfulness, and wholeness. We should be aware of our bodies being temples of the living Gods whenever we meditate deep. Just a 15-20 minutes session of meditation and deep breathing can help you feel relaxed and peaceful.

However, if you need to advance in deep meditation, preparation is a must. Many researchers and people close to the field of meditation/spirituality have, throughout the ages, found the imperative need for preparation before dwelling into meditation. Some of them think only cleaning the body with water and thoroughly washing it is enough, while others have their specific ways, methods, and steps of cleansing a body. Some of them feel that to meditate, you must avoid certain foods/fruits for a while. There are additional breathing exercises and techniques as well, which, if practiced, can help bring balance in the respiratory system. This enables normal circulatory flow throughout the body. Similarly, some people and preachers think music, incantations, sounds, or even odors can be conducive to producing the best suitable environment for deep meditation. In the world of spirituality, we consider all these features as distractions, and to meditate, a person should be free of all such uncertainties. As the current rises in the body through the centers during meditation, these adjoining external preparations aiding to the cleaning of a physical body can help speed up the process like a catalyst. They may help you cleanse the thoughts and calm the mind and body. What is the importance of cleansing when we seek to attune ourselves with the high forces? The method that is followed may not be the same for everyone and by everyone, but the essence of it remains the same.

Speaking of which reminds me that science shares a deep interconnection with meditation. Before going deeper into the discussion of meditation, let's identify and highlight some basic principles of vibration, which will enable us to understand the terms used better and relate to some experiences. There's a stronger relationship between science and spirituality, where one acts to prove the other. According to the principles of science, we have read that every element of this world comprises of many smaller particles known as atoms (further divided into sub-atomic particles). A simple object contains these atoms in several millions and billions, which is obviously uncountable. However, what science claims is that these tiny particles are in constant motion (constantly vibrating about their fixed position).

Further, the difference that we have in the states of matter is also because of the difference in the rates of vibration. For instance, the rate of atomic vibration is multiple times higher in solids than in gases. Similarly, our bodies consist of tiny constituent particles that have been taken into them, such as food, air, etc. From this, we can derive that different parts of our body are composed of different matter, with all of them vibrating at a different pace and rate of speed.

When we turn the mind towards the highest ideal, we quiet the physical body. This solitude is so silent and undisturbed that there are several physical vibrations that you can experience. Meditation evokes a new wave of senses in your body while strengthening the previous senses to the new extents of their limit. You become more sensitive towards all your senses, whether it's touch, smell, see or hear, etc. When we attune ourselves to the infinite, our glands raise the magnitude of spiritual power multiple folds. This spiritual power seeps through the body, and accumulates the vacant space within the cells, penetrating through the partially permeable membrane. With the arousing of the image, or ideal, this life force rises along the Appian Way, or the silver cord, to the pineal center in the brain. And as we know, that brain acts as a central hub for the whole bodily actions. This power is then disseminated to the other body parts – to the whole mental and physical being.

Thus, when you enter meditation, your bodily organs follow the track and respond to it in an orderly function. Whatever we relate to or set as our ideal, we attract that, multiple folds. For instance, whether your ideal projection is materialistic or spiritual, it is liberated, and it finds expression in the activity of the imaginative forces. Whereas if this ideal personification is spiritual, then you are more likely to seek spiritual development.

Amidst the rising currents within the body, it becomes aware and conscious of the distinct vibrations like a tingling or a clear vibration or motion in the body. Another indicator or another source of vibration could be in the form of current/waves flowing through the whole body, originating from the feet and up to the spine. The experiences will vary from person to person. For instance, the composite vibrations of a body acted upon by spiritual thoughts differ in various individuals. But one definite and mutually shared idea is the occurrence of a definite physical reaction in the sensitive centers. Our lives revolve around the number of basic frequencies, rhythms, beats, and patterns.

Rhythm is everywhere and in everything. It is for us to recognize those similar patterns and pleasing rhythms to attune our lives to it. Rhythm is in the heartbeat of our chest; it is in the footsteps of our stride; it is in the language we speak; it is in the chimes of a church bell. Rhythm is everywhere and in everything. It wouldn't be wrong to call life a structure of multiple frequencies and rhythms. All that we do is guided by the natural rhythms in life and nature – including our very own existence. Our beating heart and the rhythmic breath is a constant reminder of that.

Our lives and the nature surrounding it is orchestrated by the setting and rising of the sun and moon; the variation in temperature from day to night and from season to season; and by our own internal rhythm. These rhythms direct our daily life activities.

Self-cleansing: Purging One's Self

Let's get an insight into what goes beyond the physical means into the mental zone of a person during meditation. For starters, the basic idea revolves around the mind being a builder and the physical body, reflecting the processes that go within the mind.

We, as human beings, only know the 'conscious' mind that contributes to a very little part that makes up the whole mind. Contrary to that belief, if we talk about science (other than spiritual context), the science of meditation is gaining new heights of fame. The recent studies on the amalgamation of these two topics have brought many facts into the limelight, revealing little of what we call the subconscious – the storage space for memories, also known as the ever-watchful supervisor that helps regulate bodily functions.

Besides that, there's still a little division of mind that remains undiscovered. We know this state as the activity of super-conscious, or the soul–mind. This term, too, only validates the idea that goes behind this mental state, clarifying the different functions of one force. Through meditation, we seek the proper functionality of our minds. We ask the mind of our physical bodies to channel our focus in one direction by cutting out the distractions through the will. We ask our minds to center on the idea that is to be presented to the higher mind. This ideal becomes the notion behind the activity, which then has results. The help and value to the physical and mental body will transmute through the five senses, and it attunes the ideal and the purpose with the super-conscious mind. We will attain this activity of a higher mind only if we seek to understand it.

Thus, it implies the obligation of purifying our minds if we were to meditate. Then let us clean our bodies and purify our minds to consecrate ourselves in prayer. Let us be free of abhorrence, malice, materialism, and greed. Let's replace them with love, kindness, and mercy. Let there be humbleness in our hearts for it to reflect upon our soul. Let us arise with a pure and open heart, seeking the contrite heart desiring to show us the way. Then let us seek to enter.

Attuning the Self to the Whole

Attunement and self-development go hand in hand. In attuning our consciousness with the divine, each of us attunes ourselves distinctively as per our development.

Attunement is like growth, just like all attainments in the creation.

"In my Father's house are many mansions [states of consciousness]... I prepare a place for you...that where I am [in consciousness], there ye may also be [in consciousness]."

To attain meditation, proper attunement is vital. We can make perfect attunement with the ideal when we make our minds and our wills one with His Word, action, intent, and purpose. Let us pray, "Father, not my will, but Thine be done in and through me" (262-3) and mean it.

How do we know when we are not in attunement?

To be out of harmony with your neighbor or other fellow beings is to be out of harmony with your creator. The Bible says, *"If thou bring thy gift to the altar, and there remembereth that thy brother hath ought against thee; Leave there thy gift before the altar and go thy way; first be reconciled to thy brother, and then come and offer thy gift. Thou shalt love the Lord thy God with all thy heart and thy neighbor as thyself."*

The Spiritual Body
The soul

Through the powerful tool of meditation, we can become aware of the spiritual forces which lie within us. Through meditation, we may unlock the passage between our spiritual and physical bodies. Through this door arise impulses from the soul – impulses seeking residence in the physical existence.

Our souls are restricted not by one but many facets of our impression in the physical existence. The soul is always there, present, existing in its truest form. The soul waits to be put to its true purpose – a true relationship with the creator. Through meditation, we open the doors/portal to the awakening. Many people say that we, as human beings, are not aware of the soul. However, we should know that all of us have a soul that resides in our body, though temporarily, and then out of it, we go on to other states of consciousness and experiences.

The fact that we feel the sense to distinguish between good and bad, right and wrong, be sorry or to be content, the fact that we desire, signifies activities of an active mind that takes upon something temporal. Such mental activities arise from the spiritual center of our being – the soul.

The Ideal

Meditation is not restricted to one niche, nor does it have a specific method of practice. It is, in fact, to each their own. Although we follow some pre-meditation, post-meditation, and some during-meditation acts, the method of meditating for each may differ. For some, it's an escape from the noisy, polluted world of greed, evil, and anxiety into the realm of calm, serenity, and peace. Whereas, for others, it is access to knowledge. For still others, it is a passage to reach God.

With many meditators exist numerous meditations, each with its variants. However, what these have in common are the purpose and the ideal. Just solitude and soothing music will not uplift the mood and take you into the zone of meditation. Instead, if you need to experience the true essence of meditation, you need to be pure of malice, greed, harmful intentions, and the evil that lies within. Let's not confuse meditation with materialistic means, but first consider the fundamental reason for it and harmonize that reason with the strongest desire we can conceive. Some definite changes and reactions evolve within us when we enter the truest form of meditation. These reactions reflect in the physical, mental, and spiritual mind.

If the aim of our meditation is only to still the physical, direct methods should be used instead of meditation. But once you decide to pursue meditation, make sure you step in with all that you have. The physical will follow the reactions of what changes take place within, and that will reflect on your physical existence as well. Now, to fix the problem of attention, there should be a motive that serves to acquire the highest possible awareness state, at least to the extent which the human being is capable of.

The Forces

We become more conscious of the forces during meditation than at any other time! We refer to these forces as occult, psychic, intuitive, and so on. These are only various vague terms to consolidate the experience attained from the functions of God.

For example, let us consider the intuitive forces that arise from the experiences of our whole being. It can be due to introspective activities of the mind. We refer to this as "entering into the silence." Those with consistent introspection can bring to the top the experiences as a whole, and are called 'lamas' or 'sages.' An individual transforms into a master when this ability is made practical.

Methods of Meditation

We must learn to meditate just like any other task that is taught to us from a young age, for instance, walking or talking. We must learn to direct our consciousness through desire, controlled by the will.

The various methods suggested serve as an outline. It varies from person to person, depending on how comfortable they are with their own desired routine. We are capable of deciding the one that is most suitable, convenient, and comforting to us as individuals.

We all vary significantly from each other, and this uniqueness is a constructive result of different development. For example, for some, the most simple of the forms is the best, whereas others believe in performing methods with added complexities. They believe the greater the effort made, the better the results will be. However, the one thing that should remain common in all these different forms and methods is the spiritual intent, which is the only prerequisite. God's identity is of a spiritual nature, and with it, He shall be sought. He has perfected the way of life for us, and thus we should let his defined ways be the guiding principles in the formation of the ideal image.

You don't need to do any special preparations to get into the mode of meditating. All that you need to do is find a peaceful corner (preferably in the open air with the interaction of nature) and a regular mat. Just a 20-minute session of meditation and deep breathing (breathing exercise in yoga/meditation) can boost your gut feeling, and lift your mood by boosting your focus and memory. Imagine if just a small session like this can improve the cognitive functions, what wonders would a daily session (regular practice) do to you!

Experiences – to know about the different types of experiences of meditation to different types of individuals, please refer to the previous chapters.

Conclusion

Achievements come from efforts. If our aim is self-development, then we must start right where we are. Sitting idle doing nothing to improve the state you are in and the surroundings that bound you will only worsen the scenario if the present state is not yet mastered. The biggest obstacle standing in our way is the understanding of our self. Until we are fully aware of the constituent elements that make up our whole existence, we are not entitled to claim the life goal or aim. Our abilities are the ones of highest qualities, so let's not settle for anything less than the best.

The key to mastering the art of understanding ourselves is meditation. It closes the doors of the real world on us and opens them in a new dimension. Let us practice and know ourselves. Let us dare to seek, not blindly, but with faith, that we may find "the noble self." The approaches that we may use to get to that point may differ, but so do the experiences with the results. But what remains unchanged and a cause of unity among all these experiences is the same level of understanding, the same point of consciousness, and the same state of awareness. The two attitudes that are essential to attain meditational experiences are:

- A strong constant will to keep moving forward and attaining new heights
- A desire to seek the truth

Make sure to be consistent with your meditation and practice by developing a habit. Broken and fragmented meditation achieves nothing more but less. Be active in holding the ideal and be regular in awakening your inner self, as this is the fuel to the meditation.

In the end, the efforts made are well worth the reward attained. We waste minutes and hours daily, indulge in materialistic activities, to seek temporal happiness. Whereas, if we try to put that wasted time into something like meditation, we cannot just attain the truest meaning of happiness (that last longer) but also achieve peace and satisfaction within, as the kingdom of happiness lies within. Let us call God and remind ourselves that our bodies are God's temple, as for Him, He'll meet us there.

There are points of physical contact between the organism and the soul in our bodies, which are also referred to as spiritual centers. These connections are just as real as the nerve fibers and the centers that carry impulses from our sensory organs to the brain. There is a bowl that must break, and a cord that must serve from the physical body of each individual. God's greater awareness is the goal that every soul shall desire.

Through meditation, we can prepare ourselves to increase this awareness in daily life and for the challenge known as death. We seek to find God by finding ourselves. The path that leads to God is the path that goes through one's mind and soul. We need to purge ourselves to attain the levels of purity and cleanliness to meet God. We are his creation. And just like free will, He has left it on us to realize whether we realize our relationship with Him.

It is not about the ones descending from the heavens or emerging through the depths of the seas who would bring us the message of God. Instead, it is about us – us finding Him within our consciousness and hearts. How can we expect God to do for us what we won't do for our neighbor? If you are expecting the otherwise, that's selfish and not from the attributes of God. *For as we do it unto the least of our brethren, we do it unto our Lord.*

Human minds get scared on listening things and say, "I do not understand, I do not comprehend." Why? Why have we put a limitations on our mind, body, and soul to not realize the opportunities that reside within us to know our Maker?

Let us cleanse our mind, body, and soul by praying, to seek the light and guidance in our paths. Let's pray to see humbleness in our hearts, for we must be humble within to know Him and arise with an open, seeking, a contrite spirit, desirous of having us shown the way. Instead of going astray, let us be true to the vision shown to us. No matter how deep you are into the distractions of this world, God would listen to your call whenever you reach out to him with pure intentions. His promise has been, ***"When ye call, I will hear and will answer speedily."*** So, when He responds, let us open our minds and hearts to the glories that are ours.

Chapter 9
The Evolution of Mind!

It is only your self-identification with your mind that makes you happy or unhappy. Rebel against your slavery to your mind, see your bonds as self-created and break the chains of attachment and revulsion. Keep in mind your goal of freedom, until it dawns on you that you are already free, that freedom is not something in the distant future to be earned with painful efforts, but perennially one's own, to be used! Liberation is not an acquisition but a matter of courage, the courage to believe that you are free already and to act on it.
- The Sense of "I am" (Consciousness)
- Sri Nisargadatta Maharaj

The following chapter revolves around the core principals of peace, mind, mind-reality, and happiness. The chapter is constructed under the light of marshaled guidelines by Nisargadatta Maharaj – the personality who served as a beacon of light for the path of righteousness and self-discovery.

Along with the many aspects of his personality, Sri Nisargadatta Maharaj was a Philosopher of Advaita (Non-dualism). Primarily he belonged to India and spent a major part of his life as a spiritual leader. He also belonged to the Navnath Sampradaya, serving as a Guru for a good part of his existence, helping and guiding people in the light of his own personal experiences.

Since Ramana Maharshi, Sri Nisargadatta – with his minimalistic and direct explanation of non-dualism – has remained a renowned teacher of Advaita. He has written several pieces, out of which the one that gained the most fame was the English translated version of his Marathi book, 'I am that.' The book's fame spread across not just the east but the western part of the world, bringing Sri Nisargadatta worldwide recognition and followers belonging to various cultures and beliefs. The published version of his English translation was done by Maurice Frydman.

Nisargadatta talked about the 'Direct Way' of knowing the Final Reality; the reality which is self-warning; the reality that lies beyond the very sudden surfaces the mind can interpret; the reality that lies within the reality, beyond the illusions of this materialism driven world; the reality, the truth of knowing oneself by breaking the barriers of mind's false identifications with already preconceived notions of this world; the reality beyond the false identification with the ego.

Nisargadatta Maharaj was transformed by the teachings of his Guru. His Guru, who was introduced to him by a friend, enlightened him with the knowledge of beyond. He guided Nisargadatta's path and navigated him to the point in life, where he evolved into a new personality. Nisargadatta gained an interest in spirituality and religious teachings by accompanying his father to meetings and gatherings. He was a part of such religious gatherings and meetups and dwelled upon all these topics more than anyone imagined he would. In his early days of life, he used to lend a hand to his father in tending to the cattle, working in the fields and etc. Though he had no educational history, Maharaj possessed an inquisitive mind with progressive ideology. He was bubbling with all sorts of different questions and queries.

Maruti (his other name) lived a humdrum life until he reached middle age. The event that proved to be the pivotal point in his life was the evening his friend took him to his Guru. Guru handed Maruti a mantra to recite and practice, and after that, it was like the birth of a new him. His personality evolved to be greater, better, humble, and more fulfilling. It was almost as if a cosmic explosion has just occurred within him.

That was the point when the personality of Maruti dissolved and re-evolved as of Sri Nisargadatta!

As per Nisargadatta, when he met his Guru, he told him: ***"You are not what you take yourself to be. Find out what you are. Watch the sense 'I am,' find your real Self."***

Nisargadatta took the advice as a command and religiously commenced every teaching he received from his Guru. From the initial classes, where everything seemed to be vague and abstract, Nisargadatta finally started to grasp the hints. Slowly and gradually, he developed a bond of trust with his Guru, which helped him climb the stairs of his spiritual journey even quicker. He obeyed him and trusted him for whatever he asked him to do. His teachings of getting to know your real-self impressed Nisargadatta deeply and stayed with him. He began the process of finding himself, the one true self which lies beneath this physical appearance of reality.

Nisargadatta would spend all his spare time looking at his reflection in the mirror and in the water bodies to see how he was aging in the light of spiritual guidance. He would look at the changes these teachings brought to him and how soon it was all happening. His teacher told him to grab onto the sense of 'I am' tenaciously and under no circumstances to go astray, even for a moment. As commanded, Nisargadatta held onto the teachings of his guru and made sure to never lose track of the pre-guided line.

It wasn't long before Nisargadatta began to realize the sense of change that was unfolding in his body and soul. Nisargadatta describes the journey of realizing the truth of his Master's teachings in such words: 'All I did was remember his teachings. His face, his words, his voice, his aura, and his personality kept resonating inside the membranes of my brain." This pivotal point brought an end to mind, and in the stillness of that mind, he saw himself as 'I am' – unbound.

Nisargadatta explains that he simply followed his teacher's guidance to focus the mind on purely being 'I am.' He used to meditate for long hours. He would sit in solitude for the extended hours together with his master, with nothing but 'I am' in my mind, and it wouldn't take long for peace, joy, and love to start flowing through his aura, making it the normal state for Nisargadatta. He reflects upon his experience in these words, 'In that moment, all in everything seemed to just disappear.' He could see or sense no one beside him, neither the guru, the place they are sitting in, the life he is living, the family/friends/social life he had, and nor even himself. And in that solitude, it was only the peace that remained unfathomable silence.

The purpose of spirituality lies in knowing your own self – self-discovery is the destination that spirituality leads you to.

Sri Nisargadatta had a very specific style of his own, even when it came to writing, just like his personality.

As per Maurice Frydman's description of him: *He was a rebellious spirit, abrupt in his style of discussion, provocative, and immensely profound, cutting to the core and wasting little effort on inessentials. His terse but potent sayings are known for their ability to trigger radical shifts from philosophical mind-games to the purity of consciousness, just by hearing or even reading them.*

His words were no ordinary lexis, but they had a deeper meaning to them. It is as if he had knowledge of what lies beyond. The measure of his wealth is his perennial knowledge and wisdom, which is unparalleled and cannot be compared to any worldly education or materialism. His conversations reflect his warmhearted, tender, humorous, and fearless personality that is inspiring in multiple aspects of life.

Peace is in the Quietness of Mind

Have you ever found yourself weak? Have you felt not well, and wondered why you weren't okay? Have you ever tried to find out if you are actually weak or unwell? Is it your body that is unwell or the mind? Most often than not, we confuse the weakness and unwellness of the mind with that of the body. One day you are glad, and the very next day, you are sad for the same reason. Where are these emotions driven from – the body or the mind? The mind is the knower. It is the knower of what you are feeling, what you are thinking, what you are stepping into. It knows what you have been through, and the consequences that something or someone will bring you.

Everything you feel physically is a signal sent through your mind across the whole body. Whether it's happiness, sadness, anger, anguish, regret, pain, burn, fear, enlightenment, or any other thing, the brain is the central processing unit of the whole body that transfers signals and information throughout the whole body.

According to the translation of recorded tapes, Sri Nisargadatta says when asked about if the mind (the knower) knows itself. *"The mind is discontinuous. Again and again, it blanks out, like in sleep or swoon, or distraction. There must be something continuous to register discontinuity."* However, if you think about it, the explanation contradicts the idea that the mind remembers everything, which stands for continuity. To which Sir Nisargadatta replied, *"Memory is always partial, unreliable and evanescent. It does not explain the strong sense of identity pervading consciousness, the sense 'I am.' Find out what is at the root of it."*

The Peace of Mind

Is Your Peace, In Actual Just the Absence of Disturbance?

What is the definition of peace of mind to you? What actually is the peace of mind at all? Is it just the absence of the casual problems that have you surrounded? Is peace of mind a few moments of solitude that you earn for yourself after a hectic routine at work? Is peace of mind just mere happiness that you find in compensation of an end to longing darkness? All of us have a different definition of peace of mind; however, no one is sure enough of having the authentic meaning.

We perceive peace as something we do not find trouble in. But that is not peace. That feeling that you are misapprehending in the disguise of peace can be over in no time; it can be revoked by any minor inconvenience you may face. And sadly, if that's the peace of mind, then all this hard work and effort into achieving it is not worth it.

The mind is the power generation unit for the queries and disturbances; how can one thing whose nature is to be at unease all the time be at peace? Sri Nisargadatta has beautifully summed up the essence of defining what peace of mind is – in fact, what peace of mind is not. Yoga nurtures you, undoubtedly. It emits positive vibes that have an immense impact on you physically, mentally, and spiritually as well. However, if you perform yoga or any such sort of meditation exercise in the disguise of peace of mind, then you are in the dark.

Sri Nisargadatta says:

"Naturally. There will be no end to it because there is no such thing as peace of mind. Mind means disturbance; restlessness itself is mind. Yoga is not an attribute of the mind, nor is it a state of mind.

Examine closely, and you will see that the mind is seething with thoughts. It may go blank occasionally, but it does it for a time and reverts to its usual restlessness. A becalmed mind is not a peaceful mind. Don't you see the contradiction? For many years you sought your peace of mind. You could not find it, for a thing essentially restless cannot be at peace.

The peace you claim to have found is very brittle; any little thing can crack it. What you call peace is only an absence of disturbance. It is hardly worth the name. The real peace cannot be disturbed. Can you claim a peace of mind that is unassailable?"

What are your thoughts now? Do you, too, think that you have acquired peace of mind and all that you have been yearning for all this time? No! What you have acquired is a subtle pause, a subtle pause on the gradient ramp. A little push, and you will again be rolling down the hill in no time, making efforts and throwing your hands here and there just to gain another temporary pause back into your life – another sojourn point for the mind! The state you are in is not the peace of mind. In fact, it is the striving force that is keeping you going throughout the day, week, month, year, and this whole life. And striving too is a form of restlessness.

Sri Nisargadatta explains:

"The self does not need to be put to rest. It is peace itself, not at peace. Only the mind is restless. All it knows is restlessness, with its many modes and grades. The pleasant are considered superior, and the painful are discounted. What we call progress is merely a change over from the unpleasant to the pleasant. But changes by themselves cannot bring us to the changeless, for whatever has a beginning must have an end. The real does not begin; it only reveals itself as beginningless and endless, all-pervading, all-powerful, immovable prime mover, timelessly changeless.

Through Yoga, you have accumulated knowledge and experience. This cannot be denied. But of what use is it all to you? Yoga means union, joining. What have you re-united, rejoined?"

The true knowledge of mind is not taught; stop trying to look for what is not lost. You cannot find what is not lost. Your mind is your greatest guru and the best teacher you can ever get.

The true knowledge of the self is not knowledge. It is not something that you find by searching by looking everywhere. It is not to be found in space or time. Knowledge is but a memory, a pattern of thought, and a mental habit. All these are motivated by pleasure and pain. It is because you are goaded by pleasure and pain that you are in search of knowledge. Being oneself is completely beyond all motivation. You cannot be yourself for some reason. You are yourself, and no reason is needed. Realize that whatever you think yourself to be is just a stream of events; that while all happens, comes and goes, you alone are, the changeless among the changeful, the self-evident among the inferred. Separate the observed from the observer and abandon false identifications.

Sri Nisargadatta reflected upon some of his teachings and guidance regarding knowing what lies beyond. He taught about looking beyond the mere realities of life and looking through them. What the eyes see is not the only truth. The multiple layers of several truths lie beyond what the eyes cannot see. When we are asked to look "beyond the mind," we must act accordingly.

We need to stop seeing it through the filter of our mind, but to look beyond it. We are constantly in a conflict of war between choosing the norms, deciding what is right and wrong. This thinking curtails our instincts of looking forward to the boundaries of deciding where our limits stop. To burst the bubble, there is no end or limitation to the thinking capability of the mind. All that you need to do is look beyond it with the perception of looking beyond it, not through it. Sri Nisargadatta says, ***"While looking with the mind, you cannot go beyond it. To go beyond, you must look away from the mind and its contents."***

He further continued, *"All directions are within the mind! I am not asking you to look in any particular direction. Just look away from all that happens in your mind and bring it to the feeling 'I am.' The 'I am' is not a direction. It is the negation of all directions. Ultimately even the 'I am' will have to go, for you need not keep on asserting what is obvious. Bringing the mind to the feeling 'I am' merely helps in turning the mind away from everything else. When the mind is kept away from its preoccupations, it becomes quiet. If you do not disturb this quiet and stay in it, you find that it is permeated with a light and a love you have never known, and yet you recognize it at once as your own nature.*

"Once you have passed through this experience, you will never be the same man again; the unruly mind may break its peace and obliterate its vision, but it is bound to return, provided the effort is sustained; until the day when all bonds are broken, delusions and attachments end and life becomes supremely concentrated in the present."

This implies that the whole crux of how a human body operates and processes revolve around the basic principles of dealing with your mind. The only limitations and barriers that you have exist in your mind. You need to stop thinking on a preset pattern of thinking domain; your mind has the potential to operate on new domains and acquire the new horizons of extensive knowledge. The mind is designed to acquire, not to put limitations to the inquiry. Nurture your mind every day by practicing meditation to evolve your thinking dimensions. Do not just stay stick to previously fed information, go out, and explore what sets your soul on fire; what put you to peace; what satisfies your soul and mind. Once you have managed to achieve that state or that level, you won't be the same person again.

A Message Delivered by Nisargadatta Maharaj

Sri Nisargadatta Maharaj says, his Guru told him: *That child, which is you even now, is your real self. Go back to that state of pure being, where the 'I am' is still in its purity before it got contaminated with 'this I am' or 'that I am.' Your burden is of false self-identifications -- abandon them all.*

His guru further expounded upon this example and told Nisargadatta Maharaj: *'Trust me. I tell you, you are divine. Take it as the absolute truth. Your joy is divine; your suffering is divine too. All comes from God. Remember it always. You are God, your will alone is done.'*

According to Sri Nisargadatta, he believed his Master's preaching and followed it with heart and soul. This soon led him to the realization of the truth that was sitting at the core of his Master's words. Through his personal journey of discovery and self-exploration, he came to know the true essence of these words, realizing how wonderfully accurate and true they were. Sri Nisargadatta did believe and trust every spiritual guidance and practice his Guru delivered him.

However, he did not fully accumulate the part in his mind that concerned with the condition of believing, 'I am God, I am wonderful, and I am beyond.' Rather, he simply channeled all his focus and attention toward the information and revelation related to the focus of the mind on purely being 'I am,' and stood by it. He used to find himself in some other state or dimension through long hours of meditation and sitting in the silence with his Guru. They used to sit together, with their minds cleared of all the worldly knowledge that might constrict their spiritual vision, and soon afterward, they would experience immense peace and joy. It was as if the world around them (both) had disappeared and gone with it were all the troubles and sadness that lay within.

Watch out for your thoughts as you watch out for the traffic passing by while crossing the road. Look on either side of it; don't just look at the traffic that has already passed by you, but also for the upcoming traffic. People come and go; you register without response.

It might be difficult in the beginning for us to absorb all this knowledge and practices at once, but with time, we will find ourselves easily apprehending and operating on the different domains of mind all at once. Our mind can function on many levels at the same time, and we can be aware of them all.

It is only when our mind is caught up between thinking differently, with our mental focus and attention diverted towards different channels on any particular level, that we go blind on all the other levels. But even in that state of blindness, only the curtain has dropped over those layers; the word behind it is still progressing, outside the field of consciousness.

Do not get baffled by your thoughts and memories, and try only to channel your attention towards greater concerns that include thinking about 'Who am I?' 'How did I happen to be born?' 'Whence this universe around me?' 'What is real and what is momentary?' We are always running behind the happiness of the upper surface, always seeking pleasure and peace while avoiding the pain, and still aren't capable enough to hold onto any strand of happiness for a longer period. Don't you see how the flowchart of your emotions is operating? It is your very search for happiness that is making your life look miserable!

Try it a different way: direct all your attention to the level on which 'I am' is present, indifferent to the pain and pleasure. Within no time, you will be able to achieve that level of awareness. You will realize that happiness and peace are imbued in your nature by default. However, we only seek them through particular channels that disturb you. All that you need to do is to avoid the disturbance, and that's all. When you see there is no need, you will not look out for the things that you already have. You yourself are the highest, Supreme Reality.

In order to begin with, Sri Nisargadatta says to trust your teacher and your guide as he will be the one to hold your hand and take you out of the dark and into the light. Your preacher is your master; follow his or her commands religiously. In this case, the teacher is Sri Nisargadatta. This enables you to take your very first steps. The very first steps are the most difficult. The rest just becomes the pattern to be followed as per your first steps. Once you have taken the first steps, then your trust will be justified with your own personal experiences. In every walk of life, gaining initial trust is the key to the success of the whole journey – initial trust is the most difficult. Every undertaking is an act of faith.

Even the bread that you consume daily, you eat it on your trust. Nisargadatta reinforces that by believing everything that he has told us, we can achieve everything: "You are the all-pervading, all transcending reality. Behave accordingly, think, feel, and act in harmony with the whole, and the actual experience of what I say will dawn upon you in no time. No effort is needed. Have faith and act on it."

He said: *"It is in your own interest that I speak because above all, you love yourself, you want yourself secure and happy. Don't be ashamed of it, don't deny it. It is natural and good to love oneself. Only you should know what exactly do you love? It is not the body that you love, it is Life -- perceiving, feeling, thinking, doing, loving, striving, and creating. It is that Life you love, which is you, which is all. Realize it in its totality, beyond all divisions and limitations, and all your desires will merge in it, for the greater contains the smaller. Therefore find yourself, for in finding that you find all. Everybody is glad to be. But few know the fullness of it. You come to know by dwelling in your mind on 'I am,' 'I know,' and 'I love' -- with the will of reaching the deepest meaning of these words."*

Teachings of the Bhagavad Geeta about Inner Being – The Self!

The Great Spiritual Conquest

Uddharedatmanatmanam natmanamavasadayet;
Atmaiva hyatmano bandhuratmaiva ripuratmanah.
Bandhuratma'tmanastasya yenatmaivatmana jitah;
Anatmanastu satrutve vartetatmaiva satruvat.

"One should exalt the self by the Self. One should not deprecate the Self, for the Self alone is the friend of the self, and the Self alone is also the enemy of the self. The Self is the friend of him whose self has been conquered by the Self. Where the self remains unrestrained, the Self would behave as its enemy, as an external foe." The crux of this whole chapter is contained in these two verses. The act of meditation or performing yoga is the art of the higher self, pulling up with tremendous force all that our lower self is.

Only the Self is capable of raising itself. But what does this mean? The typical archetypal self, the heavenly self, the divine self, the original self, and the absolute self that also we are, gives rise to the individual self, puny self, physical self, the political self, the Mr. or Mrs. self, or Self of such other types. You may construct a list of all the Self(s) that you are – all these transitional types of the selves are a conglomeration of what is known to be the Individual Personal Self. This needs to be melted down like a block of ice or dissolved just like the salt in the water, before the blazing sun of the knowledge of higher self.

But where is it – the Higher Self? How high is it, or how far away is it? How much distance lies between dreaming and waking up? How many miles lie between the distance of dreaming and waking up? How many light-years would you need to travel? Indeed, a tremendous distance would be to go from one world to a completely other world. However, one thing that we can unanimously agree upon is that there sure is a distance between both the two stages, which is perhaps immeasurable and cannot be calculated physically, but logically, you can!

Similarly, there is no physical distance between the Higher Self and the Lower Self – the God and the Human being. God is closer to us than our own shadows, all that we need to do is clear the thick mist surrounding our vision, to be able to see it clearly. God and the Man can touch each other, not physically as in touching the fingers, but as in the higher thought, including the lower thought, the higher knowledge transcends the lower knowledge, the higher education overtakes the lower or lesser education the same way higher wisdom engulfs the lower. All these calculations are physically immeasurable; they are only measurements that exist and can be perceived in an understanding.

"Find the god in your own heart, and you will understand by direct intuition what all the great teachers, real mythic, true philosophers, and inspired people have been trying to tell you by the tortuous method of using words."

–Paul Brunton

The higher self that we are talking about, the God-driven self, is our one true friend. We can draw sustenance from the true self at any given moment. However, when the lower ego-centric self imposes its independence, it becomes its own enemy. As the apt saying goes, "To Thine own Self Be True."

"You are a Divine Being. An All-powerful Creator. You are a Deity in jeans and a t-shirt, and within you dwells the infinite wisdom of the ages and the sacred creative force of All that is, will be and ever was."
-Anthon St. Maarten, Divine Living: The Essential Guide to Your True Destiny

Moving ahead, who is he that is friends with the higher self? What kind of a person can qualify as a friend of the higher self? What are the criteria to be called a friend or befriends with the Higher Self? You, dear reader, you are that particular kind of a person. The kind of person that falls under the criteria is the person who is alone can call himself the friend of a higher self.

You are not required to possess high riches, all that you need to do is to be high in regards to personality and persona; high in a spiritual context. By placing significant efforts and some hard work, you need to acquire some qualities and let go of some of the attributes. We have the best example of the Krishna, the one who was a complete master of himself, the one who saw beyond the worldly desires, the one who realized the true essence of living.

The Eternal is irradiated through his Person. You cannot be of a high rank/attributes as long as you are a slave to your desires. You seek what the mind perceives as rapid occurring only. You are bewildered in the wildness of this world and all the beautiful illusions it has for you. And as long as you hold on to befuddling sensory attractions, you can never behold the Great Being. We are now living in a very tangible world. We seek to believe what we can touch, feel, see, or listen to. We are completely blinded by the realities that lie beneath this mere transitory world. The self that we are is now ridden over by the potentialities of sense contacts, sense desires, and sense perceptions. We are breathing in an atmosphere of sensations. To experience the true self and seek the pleasure of true SELF, you need to break down these tall walls to see par them. *"All the henchmen behind them are nowhere behind this one Person,"* said Sanjaya to Dhritarashtra.

There are numerous standards of beauty and expert creation standing in this world surrounded by the aura of their own amazing attributes. However, the Higher Self is standing by itself alone, unconcerned about the joys and powers the others possess. That one being is true and most pure. That Being is greater than the rest and the superior to the superiors; it is alone enough for the rest of the existence(s).

In the Mundakopanishad, there is a similar analogy. Two birds are perching on a single tree, sitting on the same branch. There is a bird that is looking at the beautiful, delicious fruits but never eats them. The other one is very much engrossed in eating the delicious fruits – so much engaged in eating that it is not even aware that there is a friend sitting nearby. When the eating subsides, when the bird that is enjoying the delicious yield of this tree of life gets fed up with it and turns its gaze on the one who is silently witnessing only and not eating anything, its liberation takes place.

As long as Arjuna was looking at the army only, he was frightened. When he turned his eye to Krishna, energy entered him. Very active and virulent were the people whom he was facing in the front, known and unknown, kinsmen and enemies, put together. When seeing them, there was agitation in the heart, and a valorous attitude manifested itself to fight the forces and attack them. But then he looked at the charming blue Man sitting, doing nothing. And that Nothing indeed was doing everything. Man does many things; God does nothing. That One who does nothing actually does more things than the many things apparently done by people in this world.

All that we are, all that we possess, and all that we have done in the past, it all fades before that one glorious and supreme dignity: God. Who says that the sun in the sky does nothing at all? Is it just there hanging onto the firmament for the sake of nothing? It may not speak in the audible frequencies that your mind can interpret at the instant, but it does work. It may not proclaim it, but it silently locates itself in the wide horizons of the blue skies. That silent existence is sufficient to make everything alive in this world. We are the ones who are running every day, not the sun. The sun stays in a fixed position, not running about while causing everything to run. The higher self is the One, single, not alone but single, complete in its own existence. The supreme power, the divine source, stands singular. It is we, the ones with the lower position of ourselves, who feel we are multifold. We have made ourselves so weak that we constantly need something or someone to indulge in or with. We have many businesses, or we have many relations to look after the needs of or such. On this lower level of our own selves, it is we who are engaged in all sorts of arrangements. Whereas in the higher one, there is nothing for us to do anymore, we only need to be. When you feel complete and satisfied within your own existence, without relying on another being or an object in the higher self, you have done everything – everything needed for causing the cease.

Bhagavad Gita and its teaching are spread across on broad horizons and contain knowledge about almost every aspect of the world that is required to live a life, a better life. From the seventh till the eleventh chapter, the pattern that the context follows is in ascending order of the consciousness of reality, gradually revealing itself by stages. It evolves in gradual stages where, in the beginning, one feels isolated/alone/stranded. However, as the chapters progress, the relationship with God is exposed to the believer, and gradually the bond becomes so strong as if to be inseparable.

The next stage that plays a pivotal role is the one where it becomes identical; God becomes our own self. The rest of the chapters contain the knowledge about how to apply that significant knowledge in our daily life, and on how we can implement the raw source of information in our day to day life and make the most out of it.

Due to this and many other contributing factors, Bhagavad Gita is seen as a masterpiece or an epitome of collection of techniques one can follow to blend together the God and the creation – the here and the hereafter. The life on earth is the life we will live transfigured in eternity. Within the passages of the Holy Bhagavad Gita, it says:

"Where the Absolute and the relative melt into each other, death becomes life, all is seen in the All, and there is ever prosperity, victory, happiness, and established polity."

Awareness Watching Awareness Method Steps to Practice Awareness!

Before we delve into the studies of practicing this method and techniques, we need to have a little background for the preparations – what do you need to do? How long should the exercise be? What are the influential factors that directly or indirectly affect your procedure? Are there any additional activities that you need to adopt in your everyday life to be able to practice this meditation? Or are there any particular activities that you are currently doing in your everyday life that you need to drop? For starters, set aside as much time every day as you can to practice the **Awareness Watching Awareness Method.** You need to make yourself light – light as in not heavily burdened by the worldly activities. What happens is, we are so occupied by the worldly activities that keep us engaged all the time. Our minds and thoughts are constantly acquired, thinking about the things that take up space in the chamber of our brains.

Thus, a good starting point will be to drop as many unnecessary activities as possible from your everyday life so that you can keep your time and brain engaged in the thoughts of Awareness. However, if you think that most of the activities that you have in your everyday life are the 'necessary' ones, and you are not willing, or somehow you are not able to drop them, then try to make the most out of the limited time you get for the Practice (until the extremely intense desire for liberation awakens in you).

Activities that fall under the category of being necessary for general are eating a healthy diet, working (if you are the breadwinner and your family depends on you), taking care of the children, and such. However, activities that are not so important are social gatherings, parties, entertainment, extracurricular activities, or basically any sort of activity that drives away your attention. If your daily routine is occupied by a lot of necessary activities, then you may practice for at least two hours a day. However, for the people who are retired and have enough time, they may indulge in even longer practice for better and effective results.

The next thing for the preparation steps is that you need to make sure you practice in a silent environment, an undisturbed atmosphere where your aura and your surroundings are not affected by any sorts of inconvenience. Practice in solitude, and if you are living with people and can't find a particular spot for yourself, then ask the people residing with you not to disturb you by any means unless there's an emergency.

The next thing is posture. Body posture is not important in the Awareness Watching Awareness Method. However, you need to make sure that your body is at rest and is not feeling any sort of stress or strain. As for that, it drives your attention away from the actual task. You may choose any comfortable position to sit in as you may prefer (a chair, a sofa, bed, or ground or anything to rest your body on, as long as you don't fall asleep). Make sure your posture helps you ignore the body completely.

To begin with, you need to have a better understanding of some words to help you understand basic definitions and their true essence. For this purpose, practice the following definitions for the words:

Thought: Thoughts are the words of your native language in your mind. For instance, if you are a native English speaker, and the language you think is also English, thoughts are those English words scattered in your mind. Similarly, if you think in two languages, then thoughts are the sum of those two languages combined for you.

Awareness: When you wake up in the morning, awareness is that consciousness that woke up in the morning. Here's a little recap of what awareness is and what it is not. Well, thoughts come and go, with very little tendencies of developing a vision. They stay in your mind for a while and then are replaced by some new thoughts in no time. But the background of the awareness remains constant and continuous throughout until you go to sleep at night.

You, in your wholeness, are awareness. It is you that is your own awareness. Awareness is not the thoughts. It doesn't leave you from the time you wake up in the morning till the bedtime at night, regardless of whether or not you have thoughts. Just like this, awareness is not an emotion. In fact, it is the awareness of the emotion. Similarly, awareness is neither the thought 'I' or anything that is tangible or can be seen by the eyes. Instead, awareness is being aware of seeing those objects through your eyes and being aware of the thought 'I.' Just like this, awareness is not something far off, lofty or mysterious. In fact, it is an awareness that informs you of all these attributes. Awareness is that which wakes up in the morning and remains awake until you go to sleep at night.

Let's try an experiment following the simple steps:

- Look at any object in your room
- Notice it; notice the awareness that is looking through your eyes
- Now shut your eyes and observe that you are still aware
- This is the same awareness which was there a moment ago, looking at the room.

• Observe awareness, with your eyes still closed.

The following mentioned practices are a methodological approach, or a step by step guide to practice Awareness-watching-awareness. Moving ahead, it is highly advised to use as much as simple and short lexis as possible to describe the practice. Utilize only a description per practice session. Even if you are practicing for 3 to 4 hours a day, make sure you only focus on one description at a time, starting from the first description. If you think you have utilized all of the descriptions, then pick the one that was the easiest for you and stick with that. Awareness Watching Awareness Method is typically practiced with the eyes closed. Even if some description might have you started with your eyes open, you will be instructed to close them. Once you have closed your eyes, stay like that.

While observing your awareness, just remain with that at that moment; still, without paying attention to any of the external factors. Awareness is empty, just itself within – you are now trying to observe nothing, but just the awareness being aware of itself. Below are some of the practicing methods that you can choose from. (Although there are several techniques to practice your awareness, we are going to mention some of them to help develop a better understanding):

- Shut your eyes close and notice; observe your awareness. Channel your attention towards awareness, watching awareness, away from the body, world, and the thought. No! You do not have to think or imagine. If you notice that you are thinking, turn your attention away from the thoughts and attune it back towards Awareness Watching Awareness.

- Shut your eyes and notice you're conscious. Watch that consciousness, and be sure to stay about it. Every time your mind thinks a thought, immediately stop it right there, and continue watching your consciousness.

- Don't watch out for thoughts, but rather watch out for consciousness. Consciousness watching consciousness.

- Some other practices are:

- Look out of your room and see through the eyes of your consciousness. Shut your eyes and sense the same awareness that was there outside the room a few moments back. Observe this awareness and preserve it.

- Cancel out any thoughts right now if you happen to have many. Turn your attention solely towards awareness, eradicating any unnecessary thoughts.

- Now with your eyes shut, delve away into your consciousness and watch the watcher. Be calm, and do not let your attention divert to thoughts, keep it in contact with the awareness.

- Remain in the awareness of your own awareness. Pull yourself back if your mind dwells over irrelevant thoughts.

Chapter 10
God as Our Own Consciousness!

Pine cone at Vatican, symbolic of human enlightenment, the Third Eye

"Deep in each man is the knowledge that something knows of his existence. Something knows, and cannot be fled nor hid from."
-Cormac McCarthy, The Crossing

The quote above encapsulates the main idea of the subject of the chapter that we are about to begin.

Consciousness Is Information

The focus, the control of attention and attention itself, is the key to experience consciousness. Our brains are wired to think of numerous thoughts and processes at once. However, by keeping our attention focused, we can take control of our thoughts to experience the true consciousness of the mind. The world around us is subjected to classifications such as mental, physical, material, and emotional. But it is impossible to contain something that is infinite into a finite case. By describing ourselves and the world around us in different classifications, we are numbing the greatness of consciousness.

The whole of us and the worldly experiences are consciousness. The heaven and the earth, miles apart, but are synced with this consciousness. There is only one presence, and that is oneness itself: Heaven. We and our entire environment is heaven, but in the low or dim awareness happening as the 'human' sense, which Paul of the Bible called 'carnal mind' — the five-sense, low state of awareness. There is Higher Mind, and then there is the carnal mind, which is just a lower sense, the 'human' sense, of the One Awareness, the One Consciousness, that has been named mental, physical and material experience. Everything is consciousness, the more we try to understand, the more we become lost again because we don't understand God with intellect, but only with an inner knowing, with our faith and belief in His oneness. We never need to understand that which already is in complete understanding. Trying to understand Him will not improve it or make Him visible than that He already is.

Whenever you feel you have reached your limitations and that there is no answer to anything (or not sufficient information available to decipher it as per human understanding capacity) turn back to God. Turn back to the fact that God is infinite, and therefore there is nothing but God. Understand the concept when we refer to God as infinity. There cannot be infinity and something in addition to or something other than it. If there was something indifference to infinity or in addition to it, it wouldn't be infinity in the first place, to begin with. God is infinite and omnipresent, and so is consciousness. Consciousness, which is infinite, cannot be thus measured through the finite senses.

John Lennon said: *"I believe in God, but not as one thing, not as an old man in the sky. I believe that what people call God is something in all of us. I believe that what Jesus and Mohammed and Buddha and all the rest said was right. It's just that the translations have gone wrong."*

Perceiving Him (God), in the light of consciousness, will help you understand him through a different point of understanding. Whatever you are feeling, sensing, smelling, can be manipulated one way or the other by means of illusion. But one thing that cannot be denied or doubted is the consciousness. Your only unquestionable and absolute truth is your consciousness.

I can doubt your every tangible trait as these things are and can be manipulated to the extent that they begin to appear as pure as real. Modern science says that all that I perceive of you is nothing; there is actually nothing, but in actual, it is just the mere projection of you that exists in my mind. The thing that remains undoubtful, however, is that everyone has their own personal set of experiences and their own inner world that they are conscious of.

"You govern your surroundings by the nature of what is taking place in your consciousness."
-Joel S. Goldsmith

I, the light of consciousness, am the creator.

You are the God of your own universe, and I am the God of my own. God is almighty, indeed. Consciousness is the solid, greater power that encompasses myriad of experiences we have; from everything that we see in the world, to what we feel, think, hear, smell, touch, or taste.

"Shines forever and on all with the brilliance of its own perfection.
But the people of the world do not awake to it,
Regarding only that which sees, hears, feels and knows as mind,
Blinded by their own sight, hearing, feeling and knowing,
They do not perceive the spectral brilliance of the source of all substance."

-Huang Po

God is Consciousness

Simply understand that God is consciousness. God is not something tangible, something of a material or mental or physical matter. God is consciousness that lies within us and surrounds us. He resides within us all.

We humans measure the world around us through our senses. But God lies beyond these senses. His glory begins from where the senses fail their fullness. Our senses are just a low state of awareness, a low illumination of consciousness.

There is no place where we can go to see God. God cannot be seen since God is both the seer and the way of seeing. He is the power by which we see, hear, taste, smell, live, move, and exist. God is consciousness, and the entirety of the world around you is in your consciousness.

"When I say "I am," I do not mean a separate entity with a body as its nucleus. I mean the totality of being, the ocean of consciousness, and the entire universe of all that is and knows."

-Sri Nisargadatta Maharishi

I Am the Truth

For most of the people, the statement "I am God" is blasphemous. Well, that is because they do not give enough thought to this. They take the statement to hold literal meaning, whereas just these few words hold another universe in them to be discovered if given enough thought. As per the typical definition of the conventional religion, God is a supreme deity. He or She is not just the creator with supreme dignity but is also eternal omniscient. So how come any random human being is qualified enough to claim that he or she is God? There have been many riots, and people preaching this study have faced tortured fates throughout history.

However, when a mystic says, "I am GOD" or similar words that hold the same idea, they do not talk about an individual person. None of the previous such preachers and scholars have preached the individuality of themselves as God. In fact, the true nature of the SELF is revealed through their inner discovery and exploration of the SELF. It is this exploration that they define as God. They claim that the essence of the self, the sense of "I am" without the personal attribute is God. One of the contemporary scholars and a mystic named Thomas Merton, explains it beautifully in these words:

"If I penetrate to the depths of my own existence and my own present reality, the indefinable am that is myself in its deepest roots, then through this deep center, I pass into the infinite I am, which is the very Name of the Almighty."

One of the Hebrew names of the God Yahweh is "I am." Derived from Hebrew, the unspeakable name of God, it is often translated as **"I AM THAT I AM."**

Similar claims were made in the eastern traditions as well.

I am the infinite deep
In whom all the worlds appear to rise.

Beyond all form, forever still.
So am I

-*Ashtavakra Gita*

If you rewind a little bit of what we studied in the previous chapters, we recall some of the sayings of Shri Nisargadatta and Sri Ramana Maharshi.

The great Sri Ramana Maharshi said:

"I am" is the name of God… God is none other than the Self.

And Sri Nisargadatta explained that God is omniscient, all-knowing. So, too, consciousness is the essence and source of all our knowing. It lies behind all understanding.

God is the creator. Everything in our world, everything we see, hear, taste, smell, and touch, and every thought, feeling, fantasy, intimation, hope, and fear, is all a form that consciousness has taken on. Everything has been created in consciousness from consciousness.

One of the most renowned personalities and most revered Sufi mystics of the 12th century, Ibn-Al-Arabi wrote:

"If thou knowest thine own self, thou knowest God."

Similarly, an Indian saint named Shankara from the 18th century spoke of his enlightenment in the following words:

"I am Brahman... I dwell within all beings as the soul, the pure consciousness, the ground of all phenomena... In the days of my ignorance, I used to think of these as being separate from myself. Now I know that I am all."

All of these sayings from all the big names of ancient history evoke a new sense of enlightenment on the Biblical injunction, *"Be still, and know that I am God."* I personally believe that, by any means, it does not tend to preach, "Stop fidgeting around and recognize that the person who is speaking to you is the almighty God of all creation." In fact, it rather helps us reevaluate our spiritual consciousness, making more sense as an encouragement to still the mind. It encourages us to reflect upon knowing, not as an individual/intellectual understanding, but as a direct realization that the "I am" is your essential self. This concept of God that we study is not determined by a separate superior entity existing in some other realm or some other dimension, overlooking human affairs and judging us (loving or disliking) based on our deeds.

God is in each and every one of us: we are God. And believe it, this is one of the most intimate and undeniable aspects of ourselves. No matter what, we can never disassociate ourselves from this reality of human existence. And if we do, we are basically just going against the laws of reality. God is the light of consciousness that shines in every mind!

"The soul is in itself a most lovely and perfect image of God."

-St. John of the Cross

St. Paul's Cathedral, London

You are the Answer – Observe Yourself through You!

The human mind and body are perplexed by the idea of existing as a whole – we seize to singularize the understanding of our existence. We are constantly fighting to pluralize our personalities, and before we even realize, we find ourselves in conflict with our consciousness. To achieve the utter state of consciousness, existing as a whole without being clustered within multiple individualities, one needs to release thyself of this false sense of existing in different individualities.

Release your mind into the realms of freedom of preaching oneness and individuality, so is to make all the problems vanish. What is the reason that we have been looming around in the darkness for so long? Why are we lurking in the corners masquerading separate individual consciousness, and are never able to achieve the oneness? It is because we haven't been able to grasp the deep significance of knowing our identity as a whole? We discussed in the beginning of the book, "we are all stars wrapped up in skin; the light you've been seeking has always been within." What does it mean? The meaning you are looking for is far beyond just the sparkle of what this beautiful sentence appears to be.

The true meaning is indeed deep and holds a lesson for understanding the consciousness; as soon as we promise ourselves to wake up from the darkness of existing in multiple individualities of mind, mentality, and conscious, we will become the source of light in the darkness, for ourselves and for others. We will be able to navigate our way through the realms of freedom, released from the shackled boundaries of multiple individualities, into one whole consciousness. Learn to recognize yourself, the True Self, and accept who you really are.

When we are able to understand living altogether as an absolute in the kingdom of Perfection, the joy of life, peace of mind, body, heart, soul, and security will knock on our doors.

"No miracle can ever be denied to those who know they are one with God"

-ACIM

Verily, HE, who is the supreme, who is the greatest and the purest, exists in a secret place, not far from us. If we were to find Him, then look around nothing further than where we are. However, to do so, one must be willing to surrender themselves to the absolute; turn away from the spectral to the real; from the false to the truth; from the illusion to the reality; turn away to **Turn Within.** For it is the perfect state within us, which holds infinite love, harmony, and peace.

To us, the gates of paradise swing open once we have released ourselves and relinquished our mind and body from the false appearance of separateness and division. The cold breeze of heaven awaits our welcome as soon as we see and accept ourselves to be the ONE, and hence the new life begins.

In the beginning, it was nothing but the consciousness, and consciousness was God, and there was nothing except for the things made of the consciousness, the God. And by "In the Beginning," we mean the very beginning of the new origins of life as soon as one wakes up from his sleep and see things as they rightfully are; when one reflects upon the light of revelation.

Chapter 11
The Power Miracle – Your Power Defines You!

*You create your life through the inner power of your being,
whose source is within you and yet beyond the selves that
you know. Use those creative abilities with understanding
abandon. Honor yourselves and move through the
godliness of your being.*

–Jane Roberts

What is power?

Is power authority?

Is power possession of wealth and ranks?

Is power the measure of physical strength?

Does power need materialistic means of this world to be distinguished from other things? Or is power something more meticulous, purer, stronger, and far beyond this worldly definition?

Everyone in this world is struggling to be better at what they are doing. Some are just running after dollars, losing themselves in the crowd, while others are trying to maintain a better lifestyle. This life, however, is a delicate dance between both realities. The key to mastering this is to learn the skill of taking them both simultaneously. Some people in life are surrounded by the fog of uncertainty.

Their dilemmas and insecurities constantly trigger the embedded fears that prevent them from stepping out of their self-restricted limitations (both physical and mental). People's confusion often leads them astray by the time they reach the turning point in their life, while others make plans and cannot execute it accordingly. However, whether things are going downhill or up the scale, the stronger you are inside, the more accomplished you will be outside.

Your power defines you; your resilience, strength, abilities, and capabilities make up a human being, which is you! Thus, to be better in life at anything you step into, you must recognize what lies beneath your skin – not the flesh and bones, but the inner alignment, energy, and abilities. Know your true power, the power of Self, the power that guides you – the power which is YOU!

In this chapter, we will reinforce the idea behind getting to know the real power, which will help you become better at achieving your life goals and clearing your hazy view. We will talk about getting to know yourself under the light of a spiritual aspect and the role that spiritual teachings/guides/practices play in lying the foundation of getting to know yourself and the power that lies within you. This power is the state of mind that enhances your ability.

The inner power pushes your character and personality that you put in front of the entire world. This inner spiritual power keeps you moving forward in life. It boosts your confidence, makes you optimistic, and transforms your thoughts into hopes and possibilities. The inner power cancels out the external distractions and inner insecurities, enabling you to focus on your goals instead of getting sidetracked by unnecessary details.

This energy is multiple times stronger than you think: there's energy when you speak, there is energy in the emails you send, and there is energy in the way you talk, walk, and present yourself to your surroundings. There is energy in your physical presence. If you are functioning at a low vibrating frequency or energy, your thoughts can easily be polluted by the surrounding negativity of the same energy levels. In contrast to that, when you work with positive energy, it influences your surroundings to become more and more positive. You have the power over your energy; you can increase or decrease it to use it to serve the world.

As the Kundalini master, Yogi Bhajan said, *"Show some respect for your hidden power. Awaken it!"*

If you are ready to embrace the different possibilities of how your mind operates in several dimensions and how the parameters of life are defined, you must learn consciousness in detail. Once ready, you will begin to see how consciousness plays its part in shaping the world around you and your success. It may appear to us as we are living in one world – this very physical world of experiences, events, and action, but that's not all true.

The Worlds That Run Parallel to Each Other

We live inside the two worlds, or the two worlds live inside us. One of them is the physical reality in which we exist as humans; the other world is the world of intangible imaginative reality. This is the world of our beliefs, thoughts, mind, and subconscious reality. Both worlds interconnect and operate on a fixed pattern. The balance between them is so delicate that we even forgo thinking about existing in two different realities at the same time. They are both connected, interlinked with our existence, the part of us all.

We are like antennas, catching signals, and responding to them as we receive them. We are the receivers and transponders of the vibrations and frequencies, surrounded by 'Creation's consciousness.' Consciousness is what we are; it derives the power that lives within. Yet, many of us are still living in the delusion that some external force or something outside of us is shaping the world.

No, it's all within you. And to know this better, all that you need to do is to recognize your inner power and attune yourself to the channel of the frequency of Creation. While you often experience resonance as a state of connection, resonance is communication. Resonance is the moment to moment tracker that, by being in resonance with life, you can track manifestation in a shared communication with Creation.

In that shared communication, you draw what you are craving into manifestation through being in unity with the Creation. Resonance is important as a restored capacity in you because resonance tracks the activity of Creation, where your unity with life is occurring. When you come into resonance with Creation, you respond to what is trying to be part of your life. Everything you crave is the communication of resonance connecting you to Creation. When your solar plexus ceases to operate in fight or flight, your resonance with Creation comes online, and you experience 'gut' feelings more powerfully than the thoughts that trigger fear in you. How many times have you felt something coming into existence, but you didn't know how to pay attention or track what you felt?

You resonate with the movement of manifestation all the time. You track your communication with Creation through resonance all the time. While the symptoms are gut instinct, intuition, sense, and feeling, hunches, the actual activity is vibration, and how you register the strength or weakness of the vibration is through resonance. Everything exists in resonance – stimulating the unlimited formlessness of every possibility into manifestation.

It isn't the thing you crave that is life-giving. It is when the physical manifestation of what you crave comes into form, and you feel back in touch with your unity with life. That is the art of Creation. The extraordinary mystery of what resonates with Creation. The phenomenon of resonance – from formless to form.

The communication of resonance always moves, spiraling, always unfolding in unity with Creation. Resonance is not passive. It is the communication system of Creation behind all manifestations. Resonance builds, gathering its power when the life force of Creation is building the next manifestation. You have this sensation when you are pressing to be heard or struggling to share or request because you experience the pressure of what is trying to manifest. What you are craving is also craving you – a shared field. Using the resonance of Creation, you build a home for your craving to back to. This is the magic of resonance and Consciousness causes life. It may appear that there are several factors that may cause life, but there isn't any, other than consciousness. Nothing can alter the course of life and the events except for the consciousness, controlling which is in human's reach. Everything that appears to be on the outside and in the present now is just the reflection of what has happened previously in your consciousness. Your inner self defines your outer self, and what lies in your inner self? Your consciousness. The change in your consciousness will reflect the same change in your surroundings; then, it will not only be influential on your present but also your future.

What is Spiritual Power?

Let's get into the basics of what spiritual power is and how we can awaken it to be put to its purpose. I believe this will untangle many of the complex knots of queries and questions that live in your mind regarding spiritual power or inner power. This chapter will give you precise details of each topic mentioned below, which will change your perception of life and how you interact with the world.

Before we delve into the details of it, I would like to set the basis that the 'power' we are discussing here is not the 'power above,' 'power under,' or 'power against' anyone. If it comes from the force of will or rigid determination, then it is not power. By the time you reach new heights of consciousness beyond duality, you realize that there is neither opposed nor under the power of the force because there is no such thing as two powers.

It may appear though that there are powers against being influenced, but in the consciousness of your divine self, you know that there is no such thing; even if it seems otherwise, nothing can have power over you, for there is only one power – the power that resides in you. The power of an innermost, true, omnipotent self within you – the SELF of love, purity, goodness, and wisdom.

"I can do all things through him who strengthens me."
-ESV

Build a Connection with Your Divine Self

Contact your divine self to find the answer to the question, "Where are you giving away your power?"

As you try to build a connection with the divine self in seeking guidance, it will offer you many ways of dealing with people, objects, and events. As you gradually meditate your way to the higher levels of awakening spiritual power, external factors begin to affect you lesser and lesser until they finally release your consciousness.

Your belief is strengthened when you consciously realize the divine self as who you are. That's when no one can have power over or against you, and no one can hurt you anymore. You need not give your power away to any situation, a person, or an object.

How Does Your Life Change When You Realize That There Is Only One Power?

You stop defending and protecting yourself from the things that you may have given power to once you realize the key to power – there is no power other than that of your divine self. You will feel a positive change within yourself – the things, situations, people, and interactions that used to cause you anxiety or depression or worry will be gone because you know that they can have absolutely no power over you. The reflex that comes with this realization is confidence in yourself. You interact with the rest of the world in your surroundings in ways that reflect your boosted confidence and an awakening sense of spiritual power. What is spiritual power? What role does it play in your life, and how can you express it in your life? You let the truth of your being flow and allow it to express itself in every part of your life, with every person you interact with or in any situation you are.

To Get to Know the Truth behind Every Situation with Spiritual Power

As you spend some time in the light of wisdom, you grow with time, mentally, physically, and spiritually. The time and experience teach you to distinguish between what is true and what is unreal. When you can recognize what is true and what appears to be true (an illusion), you know what you were thinking before was a problem – and that was due to the absence of the power of the divine self. You made wrong projections viewing things from the level of your mind instead of viewing them in the light of your divine self. You are no longer fooled into believing in things as they appear to you. You develop a better and deeper understanding of not just perceptions, but behaviors – how and why things behave in the manner that they appear to. You see an opportunity in every situation offered to you. This lets you grow as a person and develops your functionality in whatever you are associated with. You become stable. You are better able to sustain the feeling of peace and tolerance, which leads you to maintain a healthy balance in your life no matter what is happening around you.

You can experience solutions, insights, inspirations, aspirations, thoughts, and guidance in the light of the SELF within. This realization will unfold the truth of situations that people cannot usually seek through their normal vision. The power to seek this imagination and reality lies within you! And remember, the universe is always bringing you close to your higher good.

This enabling of better in-depth understanding opens portals to the knowledge that lies in new dimensions. You become more accepting of new facts and figures which were previously alien to your perceptions, beliefs, and understanding. You become more confident and keen to discover better ways of handling situations with many possibilities on your hand. Life becomes a wonderful journey of fulfilled experiences and following your heart, enriched with an abundance of joy and liveliness.

Use your Spiritual Power to Transform Your Life

In this context, you work with different areas of your life and consciousness that you will improve. You change them or transform them without the aid of your force, power, or willpower. Instead, you connect with your divine self and focus your intentions to change an area. With that connection, you hold the ability to infuse this area with the spiritual power of truth and align it with your purpose.

With the realization of your spiritual power, you can break free from the chains of your old habits that have been holding you back for a very long time, and detoxify everything that is not good for your body. You will receive your highest good in this area, with the continuous affirmation that there is no two, but only one Power – the Power that lives in you, your Divine Self. Embrace the opportunities of the future with hope and a better vision – the meticulous details of your understanding of the Divine Self. Listen to the voice that speaks to you from within. Listen closely and let it navigate your path. Let it be a beacon of light in the darkness. Once you realize the sense of self-fulfillment that you achieve from this Divine Self, you embrace the self-fulfillment prophecy that satisfies as being enough for you. You stop looking at others as a source of your happiness and providence/supply.

As you see the sea of opportunities in front of you, it helps you stop clinging to the past, person or the object that was holding you back. You don't feel the need to seek more and more, but be happy with what you have because that fulfills your satisfaction. You know you will always have what you need. You have the power to face the present, deal with the past, and prepare for the future with Hope and the gift of realization of SELF.

You Plant Your Seeds of Consciousness

I believe from my teachings, and what you have read so far in this book, you will plant many seeds of consciousness that will bloom as they grow with time. This consciousness will appear in the form of a more harmonious, peaceful, and balanced life. As the truth reveals itself and keeps releasing, your understanding about your SELF will deepen, and you will become better at identifying the illusions of this world. You will realize more facts about your own self, your own identity as a Divine. You can experience many new frequent thoughts that lift the curtains from the hidden secrets – luminous thoughts, sacred thoughts, encouraging, beautiful, and positive thoughts. As these seeds of consciousness will grow, so will you with them. It will strengthen your maturity levels and give you an enhanced understanding. These seeds, as they grow, will offer you bounties of wisdom, increased awareness, and new illumination levels.

Grasp the blessings, love, vitality, and offerings your Divine Self has for you. It is always looking out for you. Your divine self brings you opportunities, paves a path for you, opens new doors, and untangles the knots. There are absolutely no limitations to how much you can grow, how far can you go, and how much of the Divine Self can express throughout this lifetime.

Santa Maria della Salute, Venice, Italy

We are Spiritual Beings Having Human Experiences

The life we live in is much more grand and magical than we believed since our minds began to develop. It is like a series of events and mysteries that keep unfolding with time. It is uncertain, unpredictable, and yet still so wonderful. You cannot control what the future holds for you, but what you can do is prepare yourself for what may come. So, open yourself and get in sync with the inner flow of life.

We are spiritual beings with human experiences. Thus, align your life and connect to your spiritual power. Connect to your spiritual guides. Connect with something greater than your own self. There is an invincible energy force that comprises limitless opportunities and possibilities, and we draw from it the array of beliefs and expectations. This energy exists in abundance, with no restrictions to its magnitude. This energy serves as unlimited guidance. All we need to do is to open up to the new experiences and let the spiritual power do the rest of the magic.

It is imperative to embrace your spiritual power to attain success, happiness, prosperity, and fulfillment in life. It comes from the core of who you truly are and reflects your wholeness – all that you are meant to be. No matter what phase of life you are in currently, you won't realize the essence of true power until you have attuned it with your spiritual power. Only then it allows you to attain harmony, balance, and stability in life.

The primary connection we have with the spirit is felt, and that's why it is essential to cut ourselves from external distractions and the disturbances within to achieve the highest virtue of meditation. Setting aside some time for yourself, practicing meditation, is one of the greatest ways to establish a strong spiritual practice. This will improve your health and well-being. Meditation is the key to unlock the Truth. It will surprise you to see the wonders 15 minutes of meditation can do to change your life.

Get Out of Your Way to Claim Your Inner Power

To achieve something, you need to work for it. It's said that a goal without a plan is just a wish. That's right! To achieve something, you need to go out of your way. Walk the extra mile, get out of your comfort zone, and make sure your efforts are extraordinary.

We all have inner strength, though it may be undiscovered. Unfortunately, many people unaware of this underlying power that they possess, and this is because they are living with a victim mentality. They have made their own comforting world, living in their bubble, and are unwilling to get out. This 'poor–me' attitude is an escape from the responsibilities and the realization of needing to work. It feeds off the deceitful belief that no one controls their own life. A study on the psychology of victimhood suggested that individuals with a victim mentality have difficulties expressing and processing negative emotions such as anger, fear, and disappointment.

As a result, when these feelings don't get out, they get suppressed. So much so they reflect upon your mental and physical health, hindering what you want to attract through your vibrations. This results in a constant feeling of hopelessness and disappointment. If you play the blame game all the time, hold external or internal factors responsible for your misery (or any difficulty you are in), then you are living with a victim mentality. You justify your bad behavior and mistakes; you constantly complain that nothing in your life is going as planned.

This mindset is rooted in the repeated loss of control over the outcomes of situations in your life. When you lose your power multiple times, you lose hope. You believe what you learn, which is convincing yourself no matter what you do, you can't win. We cannot entirely blame the people living with this mindset; in fact, we have all been in that situation more than once in our lives. However, not being resilient to this thinking is a problem. The only way you can achieve something in life is by stepping out of the victimized mentality and committing to working toward it. The one way you can claim your underlying power is by taking charge of responsibility for everything – your behaviors, your results, your words, and your actions. Start owning your actions to realize what it is you need to change. This is what mentally strong people do.

When you meditate, you detoxify your body from a negative mindset and transmute your thoughts, so they are channelized toward success. The world around you does not dictate the world within you! It is your inner world that keeps you moving. You are the creator of your life, and you shape its modules. Learn from your experiences and grow with them. When something doesn't go your way, step back and think about what went wrong and rectify it for the future.

"Every man must take time daily for quiet and meditation. In daily meditation lies the secret of power."
-H. Emilie Cady

You created your reality. And so, you are the only person who has the power to change it. Instead of feeling sorry for yourself, align yourself with the frequencies and vibrations of the things you want to attract. Increase your frequency by adopting various meditation methods in your life. Once you master your emotions, beliefs, and thoughts, you realize that this is the only power that you needed – the power within You!

You can have answers to your prayers when you pray in the right way, and in the right attitude by turning to power within, by acknowledging the presence of God within.

The Golden Key is inside you, and use of it opens you up to all the goodness that is yours through Divine right.

The great new thought teacher Emmet Fox taught the art of scientific prayer called the famous Golden key prayer.

"Cast your burdens on the Lord, and he will sustain you"
—Psalm 55:22

The Golden Key to Prayer

Study and research hold their own importance in their respective domains, but no amount of research will get you out of the concrete difficulty if not aligned with practical work in your own consciousness. The deliberate mistake that most people make after committing a wrong or getting in some difficulty is that they skim through book after book, reaching no conclusion.

"Read The Golden Key several times. Do exactly what it says, and if you are persistent enough, you will overcome any difficulty"

-Emmet Fox

However, what I have found throughout these years of my personal and professional experience is that prayer is the key to get yourself out of any difficult matter, whether it is major or minor. Prayer is the golden key to harmony and happiness. Those who have never been in the state of having a connection with the mightiest power in existence may find these claims irrational. But you need to believe in just one fair trial, and you will know the wonders of what this method is referring to.

Don't take anyone's word for it, but try it out for yourself. God is omnipotent, and man in his Glory and likeliness has dominion over all the things. By the term 'man,' we mean every soul of mankind that exists on this earth's surface, regardless of the level of piousness or belief they possess. The ability to draw on this power is not a niche restricted to any cast, color, or nation; it is for the whole humankind. Whoever you are, and wherever you belong to, the key to harmony is in your reach.

Emmet Fox, the very famous spiritual leader of the early 20th century, justifies this claim by saying in scientific prayer that it is God who works, and not you. So, your particular limitations or weaknesses are of no account. For beginners, this experience might be a little vague as it fits people habitual of practicing prayer daily. For beginners, it is essential to keep their minds open to new experiences and realities that will unfold within the reality they exist. Another important prerequisite for a full experience is having a firm belief – a firm faith.

The process is very simple. All that you need to do is cut off the distractions and think of that divine source – the Almighty. This is the only rule that governs this process, no matter the magnitude of your difficulty. Do not form a picture of God when you imagine Him in your prayers. This is impossible and beyond the capacity of the human mind that operates in a restricted domain. Instead, work by rehearsing anything or everything that you know of the attributes of God. He is wisdom, the inconceivable love, and the Truth of the Truths. He is everywhere, present, and aware. He knows what you behold in your deepest desires and what is buried inside your chest; He sees you, and He sees everything for He is the greatest of all.

On this same subject, Emmet Fox added in his own words:

"But you must stop thinking of the trouble, whatever it is. The rule is to think about God, and if you are thinking about your difficulty, you are not thinking about God. To be continually glancing over your shoulder to see how matters are progressing, is fatal, because that is thinking of the trouble, and you must think of God, and of nothing else. Your object is to drive the thought of the difficulty right out of your

consciousness for a few moments at least, substituting for it the thought of God. This is the crux of the whole thing. If you can become so absorbed in this consideration of the spiritual world that you really forget for a while all about the trouble concerning which you began to pray, you find that you are safely and comfortably out of your difficulty."

"Whosoever shall call upon the name of the Lord shall be saved."

Chapter 12
The Conclusion

St. Mark's Basilica, Venice, Italy

"To illustrate: Everybody in the world knows the word "God," but there are few people in the world who know God. For most of us, God has remained a word, a term, a power outside the self; God, Itself, has not become a living reality except to those few people who are known as mystics."

-Joel S. Goldsmith

What are we? What is this life even? Have you ever wondered that the breath you are inhaling could be your last? And that, in the blink of an eye, the world around us will come crashing down? Have you ever thought about why, out of a million other possibilities, you were the one to win in the race of existence? Have you ever thought about human nature, its existence, and its roots? Are we just living this life for the sake of breathing in and breathing out, or is there a purpose to it? As we approach the end of this book, I don't want the readers to read the last paragraph of it and put it on the shelf for the rest of their life. With the help of this book, I want you to reflect upon your lifestyle, the decisions you make in life, what you deem as failure and success, and how you define good and bad in your perception?

Our life is not just about the survival of the fittest, but a living experience filled with joy, happiness, satisfaction, and fulfillment. And if you recall the beginning chapters, we defined how life and success is not the count of mighty dollars you make or the belongings you have.

What defines your life is your conduct and how you spend it. If life were all just about wealth, fame, and possessions, we wouldn't see celebrities taking their own lives. Life is about the satisfaction we get out of doing things. It is about the little details and efforts we put in to make our lives healthier and prosperous. But how do we drive inner satisfaction? Inner satisfaction happens when we think of life beyond materialistic means. Once we stop racing for worldly happiness, which is temporary, only then can we find the true essence of life. But why is materialistic 'satisfaction' temporary? Happiness is happiness after all, isn't it? Well, we need to understand that the hunger for worldly or materialistic gains never ends.

You might have the best house on the block, but you would still want the newest model of a car. But would you stop wishing once you have that car? No! Your desires will grow stronger with time to have an upgraded model of it. And just like that, from one car to another, and then another, even when you have the best one, you will then wish to have your private jet. What's next, then?

So, you see, there is no end to worldly desires. It is human tendency to keep wanting more and more. And in this race of fulfilling the hunger of wants, we lose the true meaning of happiness and satisfaction. The world is changing and evolving at a rapid pace. We are barely in contact with nature and spend most of our time occupied by digital devices.

We need to look around but not at the world that has kept us blinded by its materialistic standards. Look at the hidden reality, the world beyond this one, and the place where we find the beauty of nature. The concrete jungle has marginalized the existence of natural experiences. In today's era, the western way of thinking that entails materialism (void of spirituality) has taken over entirely. The Eastern Way of Spirit is also unbalanced and leads to the need for material growth and expansion that we see today. However, we still are unbalanced. Sadly, we have lost our sense of sacredness.

Our will to look for wisdom has dropped many notches, and inconsequential things overshadow our intrinsic connection to nature. This imbalance is also reflected in the increase of neurological diseases and immunological disorders, malnutrition, and highly addictive behavior toward technology and substances. We have lost what it means to be human, forgetting the extraordinary wonder that we truly are.

What really motivated me to write this book was the realization that there is a need for reconciliation. Humans' reconciliation with their own consciousness to relinquish the steady pattern of unhappiness and join hands with the Creator. The rejuvenation of the long-lost meaning of life in its true context, and the need for humans to find true happiness is what urged me to complete it.

However, to seek true happiness, we should not rely on the material factors, but TURN WITHIN to experience the eternal joy of life. Several reasons back the evidence of life being independent of materialism.

For instance, one receives instant gratification from buying new things. But that happiness lasts for only as long as the product does, and sometimes not even that long.

What is contentment to you? This question may evoke images of lush green meadows with a trickling brook in your mind that fills you with a sense of calm. Well, if you could spend your life there, you may find some external happiness, but in real life, contentment has a lot more to do with attitude than a place or possessions.

Poverty doesn't give it, and money cannot buy it. We derive contentment from being satisfied and thankful for a life that we already have and where we find ourselves in life. Again, realizing that inner peace is more valuable than worldly riches is a great start to eternal contentment.

"To enjoy good health, to bring true happiness to one's family, to bring peace to all, one must first discipline and control one's mind. If a man can control his mind, he can

find the way to Enlightenment, and all wisdom and virtue will naturally come to him."

-Buddha

To turn within means to know THYSELF. What lies within us? What lies around us that is hidden from our sight but is equally involved? Spirituality serves as a gateway to get to know ourselves. It forms a connection between the creation and the creator and helps us in getting to know our consciousness.

It is the measure of how willing we are to allow some power greater than our own selves to guide us to the straight path. However, by no means can one define spirituality in its truest meaning. Everyone's spiritual experiences vary depending on their surroundings and their practices. So, if you fill a room with people and ask each one of them what spirituality means to them, your definition might become blurry by the end. It is not the same as asking someone what sun or a flower or a car is; instead, the definition is 'to each their own.'

Spirituality serves as a path, navigating our lives better so that the road to Grace (power greater than our own self) is not bumpy. There is less suffering and struggle when we behave spiritually. Spirituality evokes a sense of a better understanding of human nature, our own self, and what surrounds us. It provides us with the tool of sustenance through which we can ride the waves of crisis with more surrender. This way, we allow Grace to carry us.

Also, not to confuse spirituality with religion, spirituality is for everyone coming from any walk of life, regardless of the color cast, creed, etc. The way to attain a spiritual experience is not hard; it is we who have glamorized the concept of spirituality so much that there's a stigma attached to it. Spirituality isn't only subjected to wearing lulu lemons, chanting mantras, tithing, visiting church or temples, eating gluten-free foods, becoming vegetarian, and subscribing to self-help books and magazines, or any other such misguided concept. These are all the choices one makes to boost up their experience of spirituality by encouraging simplicity in nature. However, nothing of these estimations equates to being spiritual. One can wear all the right clothes, spend a whole day at the ashram and still have a negative influence. Speaking of spirituality and simplicity, at its essence, I have learned that spirituality is the measure of how unconditionally accepting we are toward life and others, and how loving we are.

Spirituality is a living practice achieved in several ways, one of the most common of which is effective meditation. Spirituality lies right here in front of you – you don't have to visit Bali, India, or Italy to experience spirituality. It's in every breath you intake and every person you meet. Though it is intangible and invisible to the normal eye, it is present everywhere you travel.

You cannot buy it, nor can you borrow it. You simply experience it through your understanding of it. Joel Goldsmith, one of my most favorite teachers and most renowned figures in the field of spiritual learning and practice, explains its true meaning.

Below is a chunk of the Transcription from the recordings of Joel Goldsmith.

"Open to us here on earth, there is the way of human life, the human being. Then there is the spiritual way of life. The difference between the individual who was living the ordinary human life and the one who is living the spiritual life is not quite as mysterious as it sounds. Living the spiritual life does not remove us unnecessarily from our normal home activities, business, or professional activities. It is merely the introduction into our daily living of a new note or different note.

The aim to develop spiritual consciousness is not primarily to produce health out of sickness or wealth out of lack. Those are the additional things, and those who catch even a grain of spiritual perception are showing forth health, prosperity, and happiness, and thus they are living their lives better than before. We may call this new dimension the presence of God or the realization of God or the activity of the Christ. What it really means is that the same individual who one day was living his or her own life alone within themselves of their own powers all of a sudden become aware of a presence – a power, a something – mostly it cannot be defined more especially when it first happens, but it is an awareness within that there is something more to my life than me; it is an instinct, an intuition, a feeling, an awareness that there is something more than what meets the eye, something that is with me or something is protecting me, or something is giving me enlightenment wisdom or guidance or direction, even in the mundane affairs of life. It is when we are aware that there is something, and you will remember. Joel Goldsmith, through his vast knowledge and research, has contributed immensely to the subject of spirituality and religious experiences. He reveals how we can attain high levels of consciousness through practice and meditation.

"God must become an activity in our consciousness."
-Joel goldsmith

Pantheon Temple (Temple of All the Gods), Rome

Spirituality is not bound to any restrictions on religious norms or practices. In fact, spirituality is far different from what religion is. To begin with, you can practice spirituality and attain the experience of knowing your true SELF through woke conscious, even if you are not religious. I would like to explain the differences between spirituality and religion so you better understand the meaning of both. First, religion is an institution followed by many people or communities sharing the same belief but for various reasons such as to instill mortality, or exert control. Whereas we recently discussed the exclusivity of spiritual experiences to each person having their personal interpretation. We define spirituality as establishing beliefs around the purpose of life and connection with each other, with no predetermined spiritual values. Spirituality is much more centered on having a sense of peace and objectivity.

"The kingdom of God is within us; the whole of the Godhead is to be found within our individual being, not in holy mountains nor yet in the temple at Jerusalem, but within us."

Spirituality undoubtedly extends to all facets of our lives. It is born within a person and develops with them. However, religion could be the initial trigger for its realization. Another big difference between religion and spirituality is that it is a personal choice, which is not facilitated by religion. We cannot find true spirituality in a temple or a church, but within our own selves. It is your way of accepting your surroundings, loving, and associating with the world around you. However, all religions practice several forms of meditation, which is a gateway to spiritual healing.

Although most religions offer the same essential practices, each religion has its distinctive orientation, drawn on its unique symbol, stories, and teachings, favoring certain practices and abstaining from others. Christianity, Hinduism, Islam, Buddhism, and Judaism are the five biggest religions that have millions of followers across the globe. One thing that is mutual among these religions is that they all practice several meditation forms.

According to Joel, an abundance of knowledge exists within us. This is the knowledge that cannot be sought from any external sources. For instance, if you intend to compose a piece of music that is so close to your life and holds meaning for you, where would you go?

Well, to do so, you would have to **turn within.** Turning yourself means to have access to the 'infinite' through your own consciousness. Even if you are sitting publicly, at work, library, or anywhere, you can just shut your eyes and turn to the infinite. Joel further expounds that it makes no difference what you may wish for. As long as it is in the realm of the mental or spiritual space, you can turn within and then what you bring forth from within you can externalize in either mental or material form as the need may be, be it in the form of a machine, a formula, an invention, a discovery, or a composition.

But before we can make it appear externally, you have to look within for the principle, awareness, understanding, and the reason you must always have before you. Through your individual consciousness, close your eyes. Close your eyes to have access to the infinite. Another example we find from Joel Goldsmith's writing on 'underlying wisdom through consciousness' was of the Egyptian monuments – the great pyramids. Those of you who have seen the pyramids of Egypt and the temples know that some tremendous architectural wisdom that we consider important today existed in 4000 years B.C! How did those men attain that wisdom? This is the day before books before libraries or research existed. The answer is these men had access to the infinite through their own consciousness. They turned within, and they brought forth this spiritual wisdom by which we live today.

Religion and Meditation

One of the many things that are mutual in all religions and their practices is meditation; all religions practice forms of meditation. While many of them offer the same essential practices, most of them have distinctive patterns and unique orientations. For centuries, people from different walks of life and with contrasting religious beliefs have mutually been participating in Meditation practices. It has helped them get a better insight into their religion and its teachings. It has been used to understand faith, norms, beliefs, rituals, practices, restrictions, and your own SELF. It has no fixed pattern and is viewed with contrasting perceptions and varying beliefs among different religions.

However, the roots of meditation can be traced back to Hinduism as well as in Buddhist scriptures. Meditation plays an integral part in shaping Buddhism into what it is today.

But meditation has been practiced in virtually every religion recorded in history, in one form or another. Meditation is a real-time, feedback-based practice. To meditate, you do not necessarily need to believe in metaphysics.

Unlike religion, meditation is not imaginary; neither does it contain any ambiguous concepts. What sits at the core of any meditation practices is the sense of awakening – this practice wakes people up. However, again, it depends on the individual's personal choice to believe in religion or not. If you think it leads to a better meditation practice, then that is your decision to make.

Meditation is a spiritual practice and is independent of any religious belief. It does not belong to or is derived from any religion. The followers that come from different walks of religious beliefs have defined the boundaries and shaped meditation through the centuries. Five of the major global religions that practice meditation are:

- Hinduism
- Buddhism
- Judaism
- Christianity
- Islam

Meditation and Hinduism

Shiva Vishnu Temple, Livermore, CA

In almost all aspects of Indian spiritual life, meditation plays a vital role. However, the degree of its integration is dependent upon each specific practitioner, and their chosen path at different life stages. India, globally recognized as the land of diversity, has an extended history with numerous interlaced traditions – Buddhism is one of them. Hinduism is not founded by one leader, or neither does the religion follows a single text. We know India for its unique as well as some prominent global contributions to spiritual practices such as Yoga and its simultaneous teachings of the Sutras of Patanjali. Hinduism's belief in rebirth is vital for their ideology. It might take several lifespans to fully indulge in and explore all of the Hindu mystical practices, which includes but is not limited to the followers of specific idols, yoga practitioners, isolated monks, and wandering ascetics, etc.

Meditation and Buddhism

Kim Son Monastery, Mt. Madonna, CA

Buddhism, the whole religion is meditation centric. Buddha, the founder of Buddhism religion, was believed to have attained enlightenment through meditation.

While most of the prevailing religions are centered on supreme entities or a godly known figure, Buddhism relies on awareness and the consciousness of mind. Reinforcing the idea of consciousness being the primary concern of meditation, Buddhists have a strong belief in the interconnection of mind and physical body. Siddhartha Gautama, a member of the royalty, abandoned his status and chose an austere life. This led him to become Buddha, also known as the fully enlightened one. Buddha discovered the Noble Eightfold Path, also called the eight principles that identify the fully developed state of a person; right resolve, right view, right effort, right speech, right meditation, right awareness, right livelihood, and right conduct.

When enlightenment dawned upon Buddha, he determined all that he had perceived was so far from the external experience that could not be elaborated in words. Rather than teaching people what they should believe in, he urged them to witness enlightenment for themselves.

It was presumed that agonizing the body was the approach to uplift the mind and that the pathway to wisdom was discovered only at the brim of death. Yet, six years later, the prince realized only frustration.

Gradually, he understood that the road to peace and enlightenment was only through mental control and discipline.

The primary teachings of Buddhism are the four essential truths. These four truths, in essence, explain the entire Buddhist route.

Suffering

Suffering and pain are an integral part of life in every form. Regardless of how good times are, we always have an underlying feeling of anxiety and stress.

1. The Root of Suffering

The root of suffering is desire and primary ignorance. We mainly suffer because of our faulty beliefs that we are individuals, separate from the rest. The difficult struggle to maintain this illusion of ego is known as samsara.

2. The End of Suffering

The truth is that our hurdles are transient. They are similar to passing dark clouds followed by sunlight and positivity. Therefore, suffering has an end, and happiness is always available to us.

3. The Path

By practicing ethics, meditation, and establishing wisdom, we can extract exactly the same road to enlightenment and liberation from suffering and pain, just like the Buddha did.

These four truths tell us that wisdom comes from walking on the Noble Path. This road might be elaborated as a structure of eight aspects of practice – comprising meditation, mindfulness, peace, and ethics that profit others.

- Along with several minor ones, there are three basic, major schools of Buddhism:
- The Hinayana School (considered the 'lesser vehicle') – it is found and practiced in Asia. Its texts are typically written in Pali. The school aims at bringing enlightenment to the individual practitioners.

- The Mahayana School (considered as the greater vehicle) – it is found and practiced predominantly in the Tibet region and Japan. Its texts are mainly written in Sanskrit. Mahayana School aims at bringing enlightenment to all beings.

- The Vajrayana School (considered as the 'indestructible vehicle') – it brings the most esoteric practices. However, another important school is Zen Buddhism (a branch of Mahayana School). Zen Buddhism began in the late sixth century, with its order being Bodhidharma.

Through Zen, illusions that are strengthened by philosophies or conventional explanations are disrupted to reveal the truth. It influences our responses and expectations. Koan is another unique form of meditation. It is also referred to as a puzzle without a definite or an apparent answer and is offered by Zen.

Meditation and Judaism

Jewish meditation includes practices of settling the mind, introspection, visualization, emotional insight, contemplation of divine names, or concentration on philosophical, ethical, or mystical ideas. Qabalah, a Hebrew word, means both to reveal and to receive. Both a metaphysical doctrine and philosophy, a tradition within Qabalah's tradition, is a symbolic code that is designed to emphasize a practitioner's further spiritual progress. The followers of Qabalah transform their inner nature with outer nature. Thus, it is done by internalizing symbols and gradually absorbing their characteristics through meditation. To each sephira, certain symbols are designated along with specified color, number, title, and image. Meditation helps to activate the higher individual faculties and brings those symbols to life.

Meditation and Christianity

Mission Church, Santa Clara, CA

Meditation on Scripture is essential to Christian living.

"I will meditate on your precepts, and fix my eyes on your ways"

-PS. 119:15

"Blessed is the man who walks not in the counsel of the wicked, nor stands in the way of sinners, nor sits in the seat of scoffers; but his delight is in the law of the Lord, and on his law he meditates day and night"

-PS. 1:1-2

"when I remember you upon my bed, and meditate on you in the watches of the night"

-Ps. 63:3

Christianity, being one of the major religions of the world, has a long history of traditions and practices. Early hermits, the dearest fathers, established the basis for Christianity. In groups or individually, they used to pray repeatedly, either in the spoken or song form. This is done with synchronized breathing to internalize the spiritual truths which they behold in their roots.

Eastern orthodox practices use icons as a focus for meditation. Similarly, visualization has been used as a medium by Jesuit traditions to respond in a deeply felt way to Christ's life scene (from nativity to crucifixion). As a practice of repeating prayers, the simplest and most universal form of Christian meditation can be found either individually, in a group, or a cycle.

Whether expressed through prayer, contemplation, song, or study, the intention is generally directed towards the heart – producing a deeply felt sense of understanding.

Meditation and Islam

As rooted deeply in the Qur'an, and in the teachings of the greatest Prophet Muhammad, Islam's mystic holy path includes commentaries by masters and teaching practices from an array of esoteric traditions.

It is further backed by the rich literary tradition, which emphasizes allegory, poetry, and symbolic stories. The arts depict universal principles, whereas everyday activities become vehicles for meditation. This includes calligraphy, dance, architecture, geometry, writing, weaving, etc. Everything is central to meditation practices – considered sacred and expressed as a form of unity in every aspect.

The pupil-teacher relationship defines the structural binding of Sufi spiritual practices. Only those coming from the chain of Prophets, hold the authority to initiate pupils. Meditation practices are dictated by the masters and can vary substantially by the time they reach their final form.

Meditation aims to focus the gaze by concentrating it at one point. Meditation (fikr) is to keep the heart focused on God. Zikr, the spoken word, highly emphasizes as an active invocation, the chant to remember God.

Sufism is a form of Islamic mysticism that emphasizes introspection and spiritual closeness with God. While it is sometimes misunderstood as a sect of Islam, it is actually a broader style of worship that transcends sects, directing followers' attention inward.

Sufi Dance or Dervish Dancing is a method where axis constantly remains in one position, centered, and the wheel moves on it. Sufi Dance brings us in a state of meditation and remembers our center inside as a center.

Whirling Dervish

Meditation and other Religions

Sikhism– Silently reading scripture to oneself, or the chanting "Waheguru" (the name of God) in a group.

In religion and without– It is truly universal. Our yearning to connect with something greater than us, our Source, has always been with us and will remain with us outside of religion.

Meditation is believed to be that sole unified concept that is mutually prevalent in every religion. It is practiced, believed, and used to attain results that offer a lot more than just soul liberation. It is often a matter of degree to which is defined how divergent practices are to meditation. The similarity between these is what determines its importance.

However, with each religion, the approach is relevantly different from the other. Although meditation cannot be restricted to any strict pattern or definition or any singular form, universal principles can be found in all the systems. Through a variety of several focal points, the whole being (including the mind, body, soul, and emotions) are actively involved and applied to develop awareness, insight, and transformation.

I am Discourses

The "I Am Discourse" books by Saint Germain was drafted for the level of consciousness that humankind had in the 1930s and 40s. The series consisting of 33 books emphasized the Ascended Master teachings – a belief that each person is an incarnation of an 'individualized presence' of the highest Almighty God. I Am Discourses put great emphasis on inner retreats of the brotherhood descriptions. It pertains to the intensified, in-depth instructions regarding the 'I AM' that has been given to individuals. When we think of the expression, 'I AM,' it signifies we have God's presence acting and expressing within our lives.

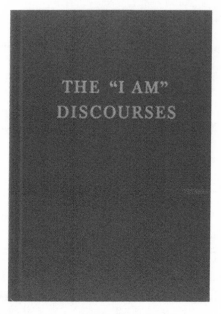

The teachings tell us that the kingdom of God resides within us and that we are one with the Spirit. Spiritual-seekers today are welcoming the true teachings of God within themselves since everything is created from God's being. It is essential to know that the real challenge of this era is not to sync with the spiritual realm but to invite that spiritual realm into our everyday life and consciousness so we can observe and practice it in all our daily activities. We live it, and in order to do this, we need to let go of the idea that God is external or beyond our reach and call.

These discourses teach us that the omnipotent, omniscient, and omnipresent creator God ('I AM' – Exodus 3:14) is present in all of us as a spark from the Holy Flame and that we can experience this divine presence, love, power, and light within us. By conforming to the things we desire, we may cause them to happen.

"All outer form and its attendant expression is but the experience Life by which each individual may learn—through his own experiences—the True Source of his Being, and come again into the Fullness of Perfection, through the Self-conscious knowing thus attained. The outer experience of Life is but a constant, changing, passing picture that the outer mind has created in its pretense (imagination) of being the Real Actor. Thus is the attention so constantly fixed upon the outer, which alone contains imperfection, that the Children of God have forgotten their own Divinity and must come back to It again."

Meditation at the Sacred Mount Shasta, CA with my husband and son.

A Course in Miracles

"In quietness are all things answered,"

"You are as certain of arriving home as is the pathway of the sun laid down before it rises, after it has set, and in the half-lit hours in between. Indeed, your pathway is more certain still. For it can not be possible to change the course of those whom God has called to Him. Therefore, obey your will and follow the One you have accepted as your voice, to speak of what you really want and really need. This is the Voice of God and also yours. And thus, He speaks of freedom and of truth. No more specific lessons are assigned, for there is no more need for them. Henceforth, hear the

Voice of God and of your Self when you retire from the world, to seek reality instead. He will direct your efforts, telling you exactly what to do, how to direct your mind, and when to come to Him in silence, asking for His sure direction and His certain Word."

A course in miracles is a reaffirmation of the core of wisdom discovered in every major world religion. The course is spiritual teaching instead of a religion. The universality of the course can be used for personal transformation by individuals of any religion. However, the course is logical and practical, based on perception and knowledge. The perception is internally an illusion because it is based upon our interpretation rather than fact. It is found in our hearts in our abandonment from God and one another. From this spring, evil, sin, fear, guilt, fear, and scarcity. The course calls this perception as the ego, which is basically a set of beliefs that focus on the body as our reality and the extent of our being.

The world of knowledge, on the other hand, is truth. The course explains that the real-world truth can only be observed through spiritual vision and not through the eyes. It is vital for the successful application of metaphysics of "A Course in Miracle" to understand it in depth; to apply these teachings to the rising upsets of your life and to experience the world one of unity, love, and abundance.

"You are as certain of arriving home as is the pathway of the sun laid down before it rises, after it has set, and in the half-lit hours in between. Indeed, your pathway is more certain still. For it cannot be possible to change the course of those whom God has called to Him. Therefore obey your will and follow Him Whom you accepted as your voice, to speak of what you really want and really need. His is the Voice for God and also yours. And thus, He speaks of freedom and of truth. No more specific lessons are assigned,

for there is no more need for them. Henceforth, hear but the Voice for God and for your Self when you retire from the world, to seek reality instead. He will direct your efforts, telling you exactly what to do, how to direct your mind, and when to come to Him in silence, asking for His sure direction and His certain Word."

Meditation is an intensely private, and a wholly personal and spiritual experience that occurs to man. It is about balancing the boat of your life even in the harshest storms and mooring it to your destination. It is about attaining balance and contentment, even in times of adversities.

This balance is then reflected in our everyday lives – in whatever we do and perceive. When the mind is at peace, we are free from mental discomfort due to influencing factors. We won't receive extreme sadness or happiness from the worldly matters and materialism but will be better able to focus on a single point of reference – our SELF.

All beliefs, faiths, and practices point to only one thing, and that is a connection with the higher power that is inside us. This source of eternal joy within us is called God, the Kingdom of Heaven, Tao, Buddha-Nature, or the Great Self.

"Ekam Sat Vipra bahudha Vadanti"

It means *"That which exists is one; Sages call it by various names."*

We are the small self, which is a part of this Great Self. Since we are separated from the Great Self, we feel unexplainable loneliness, due to which we feel miserable and unhappy.

I believe in this fast-paced world, we forgot ourselves long ago somewhere in the race. We failed to recognize that man was created in God's image or His likeness. We forgot that we were endowed with virtue and purity of purpose. The mind has gone astray from the true purpose and indulges in a carnal dictum. The secret to one's fulfillment of individual purpose in God is to be found in the evoking of one's self. To find the highest of virtues, Turn Within! Don't turn away from recognizing the perfection of spiritual spheres. Reconcile your awareness – recognize the perfection of your own Godly presence.

Resources

1. Gorman F. Paul, Only God Is, *The Essential Key to Spiritual Awakening* https://www.miracleself.com/OnlyGodIsSEEINSIDE.html

2. A Course in Miracle https://blog.12min.com/a-course-in-miracles-pdf/

3. Miracle Distribution Center https://www.miraclecenter.org/wp/about/a-course-in-miracles/

4. I am Discourses https://iamfree.co.za/iamdiscourses

5. Ascended Master Answers http://www.ascendedmasteranswers.com/practical-life/books/536-the-i-am-discourses

6. John Paul Caponigro, (2012) https://www.johnpaulcaponigro.com/blog/9419/all-religions-practice-forms-of-meditation-meditation-is-a-universal-practice/

7. Universal Class, *The Role of Religion in Meditation,* https://www.universalclass.com/articles/spirituality/the-role-of-religion-in-meditation.htm

8. About Islam, *Meditation in Different Religions,* https://aboutislam.net/spirituality/meditation-in-different-religions/

9. Fox Emmet, The Golden Key to Prayer, http://www.metaphysicspirit.com/books/The%20Golden%20Key%20to%20Prayer.pdf

10. Fox Emmet (1817), Find and Use Your Inner Power, http://iapsop.com/ssoc/1941__fox___sparks_of_truth_your_inner_power.pdf

TURN WITHIN

Made in the USA
Middletown, DE
26 August 2020